KV-190-992

Controversies
in British
Macroeconomics

Controversies in British Macroeconomics

K A Chrystal
University of Essex

Philip Allan

First published 1979 by

PHILIP ALLAN PUBLISHERS LIMITED
MARKET PLACE
DEDDINGTON
OXFORD OX5 4SE

©K. A. Chrystal 1979
All rights reserved

086003 022 9 (hardback)
086003 123 3 (paperback)

Reprinted 1980

Set by MHL Typesetting Ltd, Coventry
Printed in Great Britain at
The Camelot Press Ltd, Southampton

Contents

Preface *vii*

Introduction *1*

Part I Models

1. Text Book Models *11*
2. A Forecasting Model *28*

Part II Factions

3. Non Protagonists: Anti or Eclectic *49*
4. Keynesians *57*
5. Monetarists *73*
6. New Cambridge *88*

Part III Issues

7. Balance of Payments *103*
8. Inflation and Unemployment *121*
9. Crowding Out *142*
10. Fine Tuning *156*
11. An Example: Oil, Crisis to Crisis *169*
12. The Truth *180*

References *189*

Index *194*

Preface

The reasons for writing this book are many and various, but, as usual, largely selfish. The proximate cause of the endeavour was a chance discussion with the publisher in the autumn of 1976. I thought of writing the book because I had been assigned to teach a course in this area and yet there was no obvious core book to use. As it happens, I no longer teach that particular course, but it is to be hoped that the book will help those who teach similar courses.

My approach to the subject as set out here needs some justification. I have neither attempted a comprehensive survey of the entire literature nor a neutral assessment of the issues, based upon 'scientific' criteria. Rather I have attempted to take a clear and simple position on most of the issues discussed, as I would try to do when teaching my own students. The position taken is the one which seems to me to be indicated by the overall weight of argument and available evidence. But in expressing my own views I should like to make it clear that these views could be wrong, and indeed probably are. In reality I am open minded to the extent that I shall be pleased to be persuaded that an alternative scenario is preferable. The reason for writing the book this way is that it makes more interesting reading for students. The problem in macroeconomic controversies of the past has not been that alternative views have been clearly stated. Rather it has been that views once stated have been dogmatically defended in the face of overwhelming counter evidence. All too often an interesting idea leads to a career of increasing eccentricity.

Finally I wish to express my debts to the people who have helped me to get this far. My primary debt is to the exceptional collection of economists who stimulated my interest in economics, and especially macroeconomics, when I was a graduate student at Essex in its heyday. Notable among these are Richard Lipsey, Robert Clower, David Laidler, Frank Brechling, Michael Parkin and Edgar Feige. If any one of these is to be singled out it must be David Laidler, who not only introduced me to the mysteries of macro and monetary economics but who also took the trouble to offer detailed comments on the first draft of this book.

Many others have also offered comments on an earlier draft. Most notable among these are Mono Chatterji, Louis Christophides, Mike Wickens, James Alt, Marcus Miller, John Nixon and Nigel Wilson. The last named was among the first group of students to take my course and so he has suffered more than most. Any remaining errors were either missed, or noticed too late, by all of them, though most of the strong points are entirely my own! Last but not least my gratitude goes to Marion, Amy and Mark who make it all seem worthwhile.

K.A. CHRYSTAL
Essex
April 1979

Introduction

For one of the fundamental facts of the history of ideas is
that in general the full implications of a set of ideas are
not immediately seen.
PATINKIN

This book arises out of a course that I was asked to teach at
Essex University entitled 'Applied Macroeconomics and British
Government Policy.' It was a second-year course which
followed on immediately from a course in basic macroeconomic theory. Having just left a post as Economic Adviser
in HM Treasury, two things immediately struck me. The first
was that the best textbooks in macroeconomics were all
American. Currently the best examples seem to be Branson
and Litvack (1976), Dornbusch and Fisher (1978) and Gordon
(1978). This meant that the emphasis was not always appropriate for a British audience. For example, in the US the
balance of payments is a peripheral issue and textbooks
reflect this.

The second thing that struck me was that there seems to
be an enormous jump between the models in the textbooks
(typically the IS—LM model) and current policy debates. Too
many textbooks continue to tell us that the key difference
between Monetarists and Keynesians is the presumed slopes
of the IS and LM curves. Yet there do not seem to be more
than a few papers in the enormous policy literature of the
last decade which have paid any attention to this apparently
central issue. In reality there is probably no economist alive
who regards the inelasticity of expenditure with respect to

1

the rate of interest, or the inelasticity of demand for money with respect to the rate of interest, as the essential distinguishing feature of his analytical framework. Rather it is the textbooks which oversimplify the central issues — including, no doubt, this one.

What, then, are the issues of macroeconomics today? That is what this book is all about. It is an attempt to outline the main issues in British macroeconomics within as coherent a framework as possible. Outlining the main issues, however, does not involve any attempt to produce a comprehensive survey of every point of view that has been put forward. Rather, it involves trying to provide a structure within which the student can follow up the detailed argument for himself. To that end an attempt has been made throughout to relate issues to the relationships in simple models. The whole atmosphere in macroeconomics has changed a lot in the 1970s. This book attempts to reflect this change.

Novelty

The main original feature of the development of the arguments to follow is that for the first time an attempt is made to bring one of the three major operational forecasting models in the UK into the classroom — that of HM Treasury. This choice is considered appropriate not only because of some prior familiarity with it on the part of the author, but also because it is the model used by the central macroeconomic policy making institution in the UK.

There are two obvious hazards associated with this. First, the Treasury model is large and so the best that can be hoped for is an outline of its principal features. Selection of these necessarily involves some distortion. Second, forecasting models are organic. They are in a perpetual process of development. This means that the model changes over time. However, it is unlikely that the entire structure will change dramatically in the near future, so it involves no great loss of information to start by understanding what a particular model looked like in the recent past.

The reasons for attempting to bring forcasting models into

the consciousness of a wide academic audience are twofold. First, it seems clear that the way in which forecasting models are constructed does, in some cases, influence the way in which policy makers view particular problems. Inflation is a good example of this. The price level is usually forecast in Britain by extrapolating past cost changes. This biases opinion in favour of the belief that cost changes are the prime *cause* of inflation. The second reason is that there is a limit to the complexity of analytical 'textbook' models. Once a model gets too big it becomes impossible to 'solve' in the sense that there is no way to put signs on relevant derivatives. In other words, we cannot say in which direction endogenous variables will move in response to changes in exogenous variables. Forecasting models cannot be solved in this sense either but, because they are operational, they can be used to generate simulations of the effects of various policy changes. Thus we can see broadly what the properties of these large models are by imposing values of exogenous variables and letting the model run.

A by-product of outlining a forecasting model is that we cannot avoid looking at the precise empirical relationships between the variables in our models. This makes the fore-casting model a convenient bridging device between macro-economic theory and the world of textbooks on the one hand and empirical estimation and the policy debates on the other. The forecasters are perpetually searching for the best available characterisation of the existing data with regard to each behavioural relationship. This, of course, does not mean that the forecasting model *is* always the model in the mind of the policy makers — it is certainly not. But it does mean that operational forecasting models are perpetually being checked and revised in the light of events. If a particular relationship ceases to hold, the forecaster will be the first to notice and it will be his job to find an explanation. This means that it is sensible for macroeconomists in the academic world to keep in touch with developments resulting from the needs of forecasters. Indeed, it should not be surprising to find fore-casters leading the way in certain areas of empirical research,[1] or at the very least providing problems for academic researchers to work upon.

The Nature of Controversies

The controversies of concern in this book are not disagreements of details. We are not concerned to debate whether, for example, investment adjusts to changes in output in two years or in, say, four years. The central concern is with *broad approaches* to the working of the economy. In some ways this makes the task easier, in others more difficult. It is easier because it enables a considerable amount of detail to be neglected. It is more difficult because the central issues of concern to different groups are often different, and it becomes hard to make direct comparisons with respect to specific aspects of a general approach.[2]

This latter difficulty explains why controversies of this kind are not easily settled. It is not as easy as specifying two rival hypotheses explicitly and testing them against the data, one being rejected and the other accepted. For a start, since the difference is one of broad approach (and probably also of political philosophy as well as economic methodology) it is usually impossible to isolate a single key difference between schools. Secondly, even where differences can be isolated, convincing econometric tests are hard to find. It is possible that both approaches would perform equally well or even that both approaches would be rejected. The controversies of concern here really relate to the competition between rival research strategies rather than differences between specific hypotheses about particular functional relationships. For example, no amount of evidence is likely to convince the economist who believes that 'money' is not a meaningful entity that money might be a meaningful entity. Hence the controversies cannot be easily settled by an appeal to the data.

Controversies of this kind can never be finally settled by resort to specific evidence, or at least, neither party will ever admit that they have been settled. Rather, they are settled by a process of competition for the minds of successive generations of students and for adoption by the 'consumers' of academic output. Among the latter, policy makers themselves are obviously of considerable importance, but almost equally important are the direct controllers of economic power such as trade unions, firms and financial institutions.

All of these form a view of how the economy works and base their behaviour upon it. They will, on the whole, accept the approach which explains best most of the evidence most of the time. However, once a particular view gets established it takes a great deal of evidence and a considerable length of time to shake it.

British Controversies?

The focus of attention in this book is particularly upon Britain. However, it would not be very sensible to discuss only the output of British economists or even the contributions published in Britain. The academic community is an international one and the economic literature in the English language is dominated by the contribution of the United States — at least by quantity but probably also by quality. The main controversy — that between the Monetarists and Keynesians — has its parallels in other countries though the meaning attached to the labels differs from place to place. Someone who ventures the view in the UK that money should perhaps be in our models could be labelled a 'Monetarist', whereas every economist in the US would accept that money should be in models. The term 'Monetarist' in the US might be reserved for someone who believed that *only* money need be modelled, in order to explain the major macroeconomic problems of our day.

The international nature of the main literature means that we have to look at arguments that have been influential in Britain as well as those which are domestic products. There are, of course, groups that have played a part on the British stage but have had little or no impact abroad. New Cambridge would undoubtedly have to be so classified. But none of the issues seems to be of uniquely British interest, so it is wise to keep abreast of developments overseas. Even policy makers can read American journals, and if a theory is any good it will work in more than one country!

There is a danger, when writing about controversial topics, that the author will attempt to state the position of both sides in as neutral a way as possible, and leave the student to make up his own mind about the merits of the arguments. On the whole, the present author has tried to resist the temptation to do this, except in areas where we genuinely have little information. This is not because the author is not fair minded — on the contrary. Rather it is for two reasons. First, many of the issues are such old hat that we might as well bury them now and move on to more interesting and important problems. Second, progress is not made by 'two-handed' economists. It makes for a much more interesting book if the author's view is clearly stated. Few of the best books, or even the best teachers, in economics have achieved their success by attempting to preserve the illusion of controlled neutrality. The general drift of the arguments developed below will no doubt lead the author to be classified as a 'monetarist' in the UK, though he draws some consolation from the fact that in North America he would be thought a 'Keynesian'.

A final point worth making is about the relationship between policy makers and academics. The attitude that most academic economists have and pass on to their students is that policy makers in Britain are conservative and poorly informed. The policy maker is caricatured as picking up academic ideas with a long and variable lag. Mistakes are made because the policy maker is working with out-of-date ideas. This, of course, is a complete myth. It is true that the policy makers do not get time to do enough of their own research, but this if anything makes them highly receptive to new ideas. It is the experience of the author that few academic economists are as up to date in relevant areas of the literature as are the bulk of Treasury economists. Indeed, the real problem for policy makers is that they do not get a sufficient flow of relevant, up-to-date academic output to assist them with even a fraction of the decisions which have to be made. If British macroeconomic policy has been poor, the academic community must shoulder a substantial proportion of the responsibility.

Plan of the Book

The structure for the whole book is laid down in Chapters 1

and 2. These provide an outline of standard textbook macro-economic models and of a major forecasting model. Wherever possible the arguments of later chapters refer back to these models. Chapters 4, 5 and 6 attempt to capture the main elements of particular schools of thought. Chapter 3 is a residual category, covering a range of views that have nowhere else to go. The remainder of the book is concerned with a closer look at the main issues that have dominated macroeconomics recently — balance of payments, inflation, unemployment, crowding out and fine tuning. Chapter 11 takes a closer look at the specific issue of oil: the effects of the 1973 oil crisis and the effects of North Sea oil. The purpose of looking at this example is not to study the effects of oil itself but rather to compare different approaches to the central issues raised. Finally, Chapter 12 takes an overview of the development of macroeconomics, and summarises the main drift of the argument.

Notes

1. See, for example, Bean (1978) and Spencer and Mowl (1978).
2. In current jargon the hypotheses are often 'non-nested'; i.e. not A does not imply B, where A and B are the rival hypotheses.

PART I
Models

Chapter 1 is by way of revision. It is assumed that the reader has followed a typical introductory course in macroeconomics. The contents of the chapter are included both for completeness and as a point of departure and reference for subsequent arguments. There are three main stages of development of textbook models: first, the income—expenditure system; second, the IS—LM model which adds a monetary sector to the expenditure system; and third, the 'full' model which adds to the IS—LM model an explicit production sector, i.e. supply side.

An attempt is made in Chapter 2 to explain the major features of the forecasting model used by the Treasury. This looks very different from even the most complex textbook model but, in fact, its complexity is more apparent than real. The core of the model is a set of expenditure functions, as it would be for the simplest possible macro-model. However, UK forecasting models are evolving fast and have come a long way in the last decade.

1

Text Book Models

A thing may look specious in theory and yet be
ruinous in practice; a thing may look evil in
theory, and yet be in practice excellent.
BURKE

The role of a model is to enable the economist to isolate the
principal relationships between economic variables and to
explore the logical consequences of changing these relationships. Textbook models start with a small number of simple
relationships. Others are later added, in order to increase the
realism of the model. How realistic any particular model is
is largely a matter of judgement. The major controversies in
macroeconomics are exactly about what constitutes a satisfactory model.

Most economists trained in the last twenty years will have
been taught at least one of the models outlined below. When
asked a question about the working of the economy, they
will automatically structure their thought in terms of one of
these models. The simple expenditure system and the IS—LM
model should be familiar to all economists, though the full
model with a supply side may be less so. These models provide
a benchmark for the rest of the book. Of central concern
throughout are the main channels of causation rather than
the precise form of individual relationships.

Model I: The Expenditure System

This is the most familiar of all macro-models. It consists of an

11

accounting identity and a number of equations determining various components of national expenditure. For the most part simple linear relationships will be presumed.

1.1 $$Y \equiv C + I + G + X - P$$

National income, Y, is identically equal to consumption, C, plus investment, I, plus government expenditure, G, plus exports, X, minus imports, P.

1.2 $$C = \alpha + \beta (Y - T)$$

Consumption expenditure, C, depends upon disposable income (national income, Y, minus taxes, T).

1.3 $$P = \gamma Y$$

Imports, P, are proportional to national income, Y.

1.4 $$X = X_0$$

Exports, X, are exogenously determined.

1.5 $$G = G_0$$

Government expenditure, G, is exogenously determined.

1.6 $$I = I_0$$

Investment, I, is exogenously determined.

If tax revenue is also assumed to be fixed in size, the model is 'solved' by substituting equations 1.2–1.6 into 1.1, to yield:

1.7 $$Y = \frac{\alpha + I_0 + G_0 + X_0 - \beta T}{1 - \beta + \gamma}$$

This is the familiar 'multiplier' equation. The multiplier tells us how much national income changes in response to changes in exogenous expenditures. Its value depends upon the size of 'leakages' from the circular flow of income; notably, in this case, the marginal propensity to save, $1-\beta$, and the marginal (and average) propensity to import, γ.

All the action in this model comes from changes in exogenous expenditures. It is presumed that there are unemployed resources so output is entirely demand-determined. Supply factors are passive and do not enter into the determination of national income. Thus the chain of causation in this model leads from exogenous expenditures through the multiplier to national income.

This simple framework is, however, sufficient to explain the essence of the so-called Keynesian revolution. National income could settle at an 'equilibrium' in the presence of unemployed resources. This would happen if exogenous expenditures were insufficient to generate the full employment level of output. The simple solution is that government expenditure should be used, in conjunction with taxes, to stimulate the economy in times of depression and 'deflate' the economy when it is 'overheated.' This, in a nutshell, is the intellectual basis of countercyclical budgetary policy.

Model I is encaptured diagrammatically in figure 1.1. The $45°$ line represents the accounting identity, or aggregate supply, since it represents points where domestic expenditure and output are equal. The C and P lines represent the con-

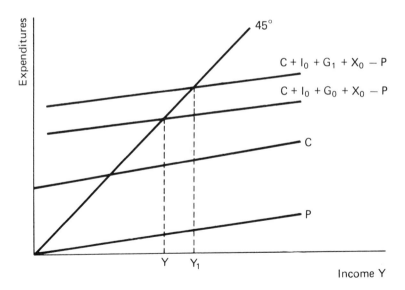

Figure 1.1 The expenditure system

sumption and import functions respectively. Aggregate domestic demand is given by $C + I_0 + X_0 - P$. This determines an equilibrium level of national income (or output) Y. An increase of income and, therefore, of employment can be achieved by increasing government expenditure, G, to G_1. Aggregate demand thereby rises to $C + I_0 + G_1 + X_0 - P$ and income rises to Y_1. Budgetary policy, that is changes in G and T, can thus be used to regulate the level of activity in the economy.

This is the first model learned by anyone who studies macroeconomics; it is, therefore, unnecessary to dwell upon it. However, a number of points should be made which will be referred to later. The first is that all the variables in the model are in 'real' terms, i.e. they are deflated by an appropriate price index. Thus inflation has no effect, since it shifts no relationship relative to another. It is common to talk of the existence of an 'inflationary gap' where aggregate expenditure exceeds aggregate output at full employment, but inflation would do nothing in this model to resolve such inconsistency.

Second, the model has nothing to say about the supply side of the economy. It is, in fact, presumed that resources are underemployed so that it is sufficient to look at *aggregate expenditure* in order to explain the determination of national output. National output is demand-determined. Obviously this has some relevance to deep depressions, but it is of questionable value in the present scene. If expenditure exceeds output at 'full employment' the model becomes indeterminate. Finally, it is clear that if the workings of this economy are to be accurately predicted then the major intellectual effort has to go into the correct specification of the various expenditure functions, the consumption function being the most 'important' of these in terms of the proportion of total expenditure involved.

Model II: The Money Augmented Expenditure System: IS–LM

Model I was sufficient to explain the essence of the Keynesian revolution, but it was not the model of Keynes' *General Theory of Employment, Interest and Money*. One interpretation of this offered by Hicks (1937) included a stylised monetary sector. The monetary sector has two assets, money and bonds, the supply and demand for which determine 'the' interest rate, since the interest rate is the yield on bonds. Interest rate changes affect real expenditures through investment behaviour, which is presumed to be interest-sensitive. A reverse link from the expenditure sector to money arises because the demand for money for transactions purposes increases with the level of income. Thus equation 1.6 now becomes:

1.8 $\quad I = \delta - \epsilon r$

Investment depends inversely on the interest rate.

and in addition we have equations for the demand for and supply of money.

1.9 $\quad M_d = \zeta Y - \eta r$

Money demand increases with income and falls with the interest rate.

1.10 $\quad M_s = M_0$

Money supply is exogenously given.

The interest rate affects the demand for money because it is the opportunity cost of holding money. (Keynes' speculative demand depended on inelastic expectations but the model works in the same way.) There is no need to specify bond market equations because any financial wealth not held in money must be held in bonds. So demand for bonds is just the inverse of the demand for money.

The money market can be characterised as in figure 1.2 where the money demand line is drawn for a given Y. The M_d line traces the relation between r and money demand, or speculative demand. At higher levels of Y the M_d line shifts up because more money is demanded for transactions purposes. Thus for a given money supply higher levels of Y will be

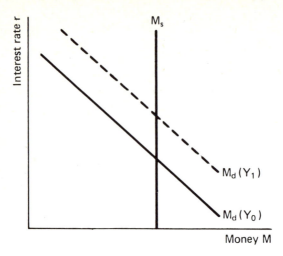

Figure 1.2 The money market

associated with higher levels of the interest rate, r. In the expenditure sector higher interest rates produce lower levels of income Y. This is because the increased interest rate reduces investment, which through the multiplier process reduces income.

Thus, we cannot solve the monetary sector or the expenditure sector separately since the outcome in each affects the other. The procedure adopted is to trace out two loci of combinations of interest rates and income which are associated with equilibrium in each sector separately. Where these two lines cross, the values of Y and r so determined will be equilibrium values for the model as a whole. In figure 1.3 the line LM is made up of combinations of Y and r that are associated with equilibrium in the money market (i.e. demand and supply of money are equal) and the line IS is made up of combinations of Y and r associated with equilibrium in the expenditure sector (i.e. injections equal withdrawals). The IS and LM curves are derived algebraically in the Appendix to this chapter.

This model still has variables determined in real terms. The money price level does not change, so changes in Y are changes in real output. It is, however, possible to allow changes in the

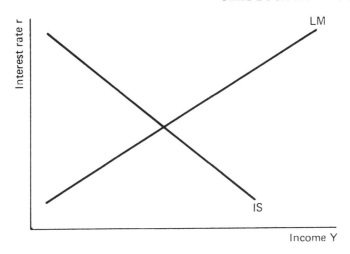

Figure 1.3

price level but only at the expense of fixing real income Y, say at full employment. Then Y is no longer a variable and p is introduced in the money demand equation which now becomes:

1.11 $\quad \dfrac{M_d}{p} = \zeta \bar{Y} - \eta r$

Real money demand depends upon the interest rate with income fixed.

The change arises because, whereas the money supply is nominal (money money), money is demanded for its real purchasing power. Thus a rise in the price level reduces the *real* money supply. For a given real income the interest rate equating money demand and supply will be higher for a higher price level and for a given *nominal* money supply. To see this, re-label the horizontal axis in figure 1.2 M/p and shift the M_s line to the left. For a given M_s, M_s/p gets smaller as p rises.

The relevance of this modification to the model will appear below but it does illustrate one case of interest. If, when full-employment real output is fixed, the money supply is increased, the net result will be an increase in the price level proportional to the increase in M. This is the classical quantity theory result and it arises because all the real variables in the system are assumed to be fixed. As a result there can be only one real money stock, in equilibrium. An increase in the nominal money stock will be eroded by a rise in prices until the real money stock of the initial situation has been restored. However, this tells us nothing about the rate of inflation since we have a comparative static model not a dynamic one. We know that a once-and-for-all rise in the money supply will produce a once-and-for-all rise in the price level, but we cannot say what the time path of this adjustment will be.

Returning to the model where real income is variable and prices are fixed, it is worth noting how monetary factors influence real behaviour. A change in the money supply does not directly influence expenditures. Rather, it leads first of all to a readjustment of portfolios. An excess supply of money is an excess demand for bonds. This leads to a rise in the price of bonds, which is equivalent to a fall in the rate of interest, since the bonds are perpetuities. Only in so far as expenditures (of any kind) are interest-sensitive will there then be any real changes in response to the initial money supply increase. An important point is involved here since some researchers in the UK have found it difficult to pick up interest effects in the aggregate investment relationship (save for housing) and have thus concluded that money is of little importance. It is quite possible, however, that the link from money to expenditure is more direct. An excess money supply could be spent, not just on bonds, but also on goods (including durable goods, viz. the property boom of 1972). In this case the link would be much more direct.

There are a number of theoretical difficulties which arise when trying to specify equations for expenditure flows when asset stocks are explicitly incorporated. Intertemporal choice theory becomes difficult to avoid. Nonetheless this line of thought has become sufficiently influential that financial asset stocks were at one time to be found in the Treasury Model (HMT) consumption equation. This change appeared in the February 1977 version of HMT, though as we shall see, the form of that equation was changed again in 1978.

Model III: Aggregate Demand and Supply

The third commonly used model adds a supply side to the economy. Models I and II are essentially ways of explaining aggregate expenditures. The addition is now made of a productive sector within which the level of employment is determined as well as the level of real output. It is effectively assumed that the capital stock is fixed. There is, therefore, a production function relating output to the input of the variable factor (labour).

Labour is hired up to the point where the value of the marginal product of labour is equal to the wage rate, and the supply of labour is also assumed to depend upon the wage rate.

1.12 $Y = f(K, L)$

Output is a function of capital and labour.

1.13 $L_d = \theta(w)$

Labour demand depends upon the wage rate.

1.14 $L_s = \lambda(w)$

Labour supply depends upon the wage rate.

The equilibrium in this sector can be illustrated with regard to labour demand and supply alone (see figure 1.4). Two important points need to be stressed. Firstly, increases in employment will be uniquely associated with increases in real national output and vice versa. This is because we have a given production function (1.12) in which labour is the only variable input. Secondly, we need to consider whether the labour demand and supply curves depend upon the money wage rate or upon the real wage rate, i.e. the money wage rate deflated by the price index of output.

A moment's thought should make it clear that firms should only be interested in the real wage rate. If the price of output and the money wage rate increased together then the levels of real output and employment at which the money wage is equal to the value of the marginal product of labour will be

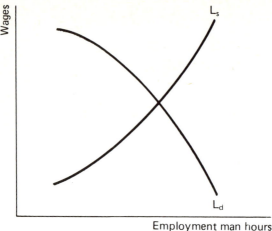

Figure 1.4

unchanged. Thus it is reasonable to presume that the *demand* for labour depends upon the real wage. So far as the supply of labour is concerned it would be rational if this depended upon the real wage since leisure is effectively forfeited for *the goods that wages will buy*. However, it is sometimes assumed that workers do not fully appreciate or anticipate the extent to which money wage increases are offset by price increases. Accordingly, it is worth pursuing two alternative assumptions with regard to labour supply. The first is that labour supply depends upon the real wage and the second is that it depends upon the money wage or, equivalently, that workers offer labour based upon the *expected* price level and expectations lag behind the reality.

If both labour demand and supply depend upon the real wage then output and employment will be determined independently of nominal prices and wages. An increase in the price of output, accompanied by a rise in money wages, would have no real effect since the real wage would not change. However, if labour supply depended upon the money wage, an increase in money wages accompanied by a proportionate rise in prices would increase labour supply. In this case both prices and real output would rise. Workers would, in effect, be suffering from the *illusion* that their real wages had risen

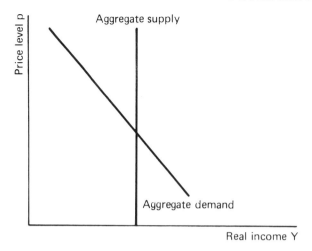

Figure 1.5

and would be acting *as if* labour supply depended upon the money wage.

It is now possible to derive what can be called aggregate demand and supply curves with both the price level *and* real income as endogenous variables. The aggregate supply curve is implicit in what has just been discussed. In the case in which labour supply depends upon the real wage, varying the price of output will leave the *real* value of output unchanged. Nothing concrete in the productive sector changes because all nominal values (i.e. prices expressed in terms of the numeraire, money) move together, and there is no change in relative prices. Here the aggregate supply curve, figure 1.5, is vertical since output is fixed independently of prices.

The situation is very different when labour supply is an increasing function of money wages, or workers act on price expectations which are incorrect. Now *any* rise in money wages is perceived as an increase in real wages so more labour is offered. If prices rise but money wages rise less fast, there will be an increase in labour supply (money wage has risen) and at the same time an increase in quantity of labour demanded (real wage has fallen). Thus there will be an increase in employment and of real output. In short, on the assumption that there is some money illusion on the labour supply side, as prices rise there will be an increase in supply of output. The aggregate supply curve will be positively sloped. This version we call Model IIIA. Let the vertical aggregate supply be Model IIIB. The latter can be thought of as the long-run situation when workers come to anticipate the price level correctly. The former can be thought of as the short-run case when price rises are not fully anticipated.

Derivation of the aggregate demand curve is entirely from the money augmented expenditure system Model II (see the Appendix to this chapter). It was noted earlier that Model II could be used to determine either real income or the price level but not both. However, it should now be noted that, for given values of all the exogenous variables (especially the nominal money supply), a higher price level will be associated with a lower level of real income. This is not because a higher price reduces the quantity demanded as in a single market demand situation. Rather, it is because, for a given nominal money supply, a higher price level reduces the real money supply. As a result the LM curve shifts to the left, the interest rate rises and real expenditures fall. Real income, therefore, falls. Thus, the aggregate demand curve, drawn between the price level and real income, is negatively sloped, figure 1.5. Higher price levels are associated with lower levels of real income *when Model II is considered alone.*

A simple example will serve to illustrate how the full model works. Anything which in Model II would have shifted the IS curve to the right or the LM curve to the right will shift the aggregate demand curve to the right, i.e. an increase in exogenous expenditures or an increase in the money supply. Only an increase in the supply of factors of production or a technical change in the production will shift the aggregate supply curve to the right. Consider then an increase in exogenous investment in figure 1.6. The upper half of the diagram shows the IS and LM curves, the lower half shows the aggregate demand and supply curves.

The initial effect of an increase in investment is to shift the IS curve to the right, IS_0 to IS_1. In Model I, income would increase as a result of the simple multiplier to Y_3. In Model II the increase in income is less than this because the increase in income raises transactions demand for money and, there-

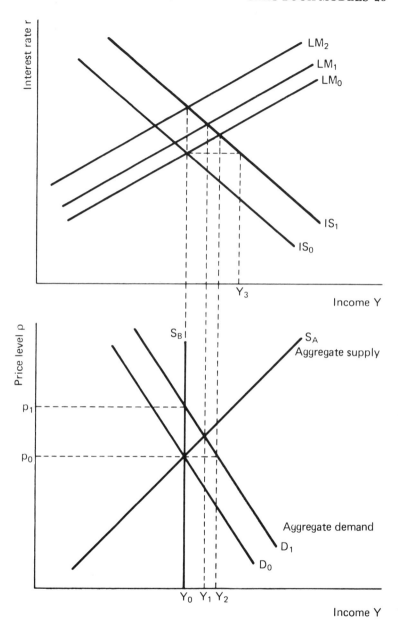

Figure 1.6 The full model

fore, bids up the interest rate. This increase in the interest rate reduces endogenous investment, which in turn reduces income. Thus in Model II income increases to Y_2 ($Y_2 < Y_3$).

Y_2 would only be the outcome in Model III if the aggregate supply curve were horizontal, i.e. if all the output demanded were forthcoming at a fixed price level. It has been seen above that this is not likely. For the money illusion or short-run case there will be some increase in both the price level and real output. The aggregate supply curve in this case is S_A. National income will rise to Y_1. This is smaller again than Y_2. The reason for this is that the increase in the price level has reduced the *real* money supply so the LM curve has shifted to LM_1, thereby increasing the interest rate and reducing endogenous expenditures still further.

Where the aggregate supply curve is vertical, S_B (i.e. the long-run case where there is no money illusion on the labour supply side) there is no increase in real national income or output. It stays at Y_0. In this case, the initial increase in exogenous expenditure leads only to a rise in the price level, from p_0 to p_1. As a result the LM curve shifts to LM_2 such that its intersection with IS_1 is at exactly the original level of real income.

Each new model in this chapter represents an extension to the previous one. The above example shows clearly how the predictions change as we move from one model to another. For a given shift in exogenous variables, Model I predicts the greatest effect on real income, since *real* variables are the only ones to adjust. Model II reduces the real effects by adding an interest rate feedback. Model IIIA reduces the real effects still further by adding a price level feedback. Finally, in Model IIIB, real effects are entirely eliminated and the adjustment is entirely in terms of the price level, interest rates and other *nominal* values.

To anticipate what is to come below, it is clear that Monetarists believe in something closer to Model IIIB while Keynesians have been largely associated with Model I. However, before turning to the points of controversy it is useful to take a look at the structure of models that are actually used to forecast the economy. Some of the methods used by forecasters turn out, themselves, to influence the way in which some policy makers view the economy. So it is useful to have a broad idea of the structure of the model in terms of which the official forecasts are constructed.

Appendix

In this Appendix a derivation is offered of the IS and LM curves as well as of the aggregate demand curve. For simplicity we take a closed economy with no government sector. There are three equations for the aggregate expenditure sector and two for the monetary sector. These are given a simple linear form.

1a.1 $Y = C + I$

1a.2 $C = \alpha + \beta Y$

1a.3 $I = \delta - \epsilon r$

These are the accounting identity, the consumption function and the investment function. Notation is standard and as in the chapter. The IS curve is derived by substituting for C and I into 1a.1. Thus

$$Y = \alpha + \beta Y + \delta - \epsilon r$$

$$Y - \beta Y = \alpha + \delta - \epsilon r$$

$$Y(1-\beta) = \alpha + \delta - \epsilon r$$

1a.4
$$\boxed{Y = \frac{\alpha}{1-\beta} + \frac{\delta}{1-\beta} - \frac{\epsilon}{1-\beta}\, r}$$

This is the IS curve. It shows a negative relationship between national income Y and the interest rate r. Notice also that an exogenous shift in consumption, α, or investment, δ, will shift the IS curve parallel to itself by the simple multiplier distance, $1/(1-\beta)$. The only difference that adding the government

sector and foreign trade would make would be to add exogenous expenditures — government expenditure and exports
— and the multiplier would become $1/[1-\beta(1-t)+\gamma]$, where
t is the income tax rate and γ is the marginal propensity to
import.

The monetary sector is very simple.

1a.5 $\quad M_s = \bar{M}$

1a.6 $\quad \dfrac{M_d}{p} = \zeta Y - \eta r$

Money supply, M_s, is exogenously determined by the authorities and demand for real money balances depends upon
income and the rate of interest. Rewrite 1a.6 as

$$M_d = p\,(\zeta Y - \eta r)$$

Set money demand equal to money supply

$$\bar{M} = p\,(\zeta Y - \eta r)$$

1a.7 $\quad \boxed{Y = \dfrac{\bar{M}}{\zeta p} + \dfrac{\eta}{\zeta}\, r}$

This is the LM curve. It expresses a positive relationship
between Y and r, and it shifts as either the money stock $\bar{M}$ or
the price level p changes. What we now have are two simultaneous equations in two unknowns Y and r. Notice that in
1a.7 the price level appears and is implicitly being held
constant.

The aggregate demand curve tells us how changes in Y and
p are related. Rearrange 1a.7 as an expression for r; substitute
this into 1a.4. This gives

$$Y = \frac{\alpha}{1-\beta} + \frac{\delta}{1-\beta} - \frac{\epsilon \zeta Y}{(1-\beta)\eta} + \frac{\epsilon \bar{M}}{p\eta(1-\beta)}$$

The solution for Y is then

1a.8

$$Y = \frac{\alpha}{(1-\beta) + \frac{\epsilon\zeta}{\eta}} + \frac{\delta}{(1-\beta) + \frac{\epsilon\zeta}{\eta}} + \frac{\epsilon\bar{M}}{p[\eta(1-\beta) + \epsilon\zeta]}$$

This is the aggregate demand curve. A higher level of p will be associated with a lower level of equilibrium, Y. Notice that since this is essentially the 'solution' of the IS–LM system, the effect of exogenous expenditures on Y is now reduced because the 'multiplier' now includes feedback from the monetary sector $\epsilon\zeta/\eta$ as well as marginal expenditure leakages $(1-\beta)$.

2

A Forecasting Model

Thine was the prophet's vision, thine
The exultation, the divine
Insanity of noble minds,
That never falters nor abates,
But labors and endures and waits,
Till all that it foresees it finds,
Or what it cannot find creates!
LONGFELLOW

Textbook models are designed to illustrate in heuristic fashion the main lines along which a macro-economy may work. They are, thus, highly aggregated and can make many simplifying assumptions in order to avoid the clutter of detail which exists in reality. Forecasters, however, must choose the level of aggregation both in the light of the level at which stable empirical relationships can be found and so that they may answer all the questions required of them. As a result of this, forecasting models are, almost universally, less aggregated than textbook models and give the superficial impression of being much more complex.

The purpose of this chapter is to attempt a sketch of the structure of a major forecasting model. This will necessarily be an oversimplification, but it is to be hoped that this introduction will encourage the student to take a look at the complete models for himself. The exposition will concentrate on the model used by the Treasury (HMT) and published as a technical manual in June 1978. It has to be admitted that this model will change over time, but most changes are likely to be of detail rather than of overall structure. The structure of the Treasury model does not differ dramatically from other major forecasting models of the UK economy, notably those of the National Institute (NI) and the London Business School (LBS), though these are two typically less disaggregated, and the latter approaches the forecasting of inflation in a different way. A brief description of these models is available in Laury, Lewis and Ormerod (1978).

HMT is a model running to about 500 equations and its complete exposition requires a volume which exceeds this entire book in size. So, in order to convey the flavour of such a model within the bounds of one brief chapter, it is necessary to select the main behavioural relationships for exposition and refer to the role of the remainder in only general terms. It should, therefore, be realised that selection involves some distortion and the following treatment represents a caricature of the truth. Nonetheless, some sketch is obviously necessary if such models are ever to enter the domain of general discussion and study for all but the forecasters themselves.

It is convenient to divide HMT up into major sections or blocks — indeed, it is published that way. For the most part, these blocks correspond to the major components of aggregate expenditure as defined in Model I above. However, now there are typically a number of sub-components to each expenditure category.

Consumption

The equation, or equations, which explain personal consumption play a prominent part in all macroeconomic models. The aggregate consumption function is indeed the relationship which has been the most intensively researched in the last thirty years. Waves of interest have typically been stimulated by the failure of the previous 'best' equation to anticipate developments in events. The first two published versions of HMT contained a simple permanent income formulation.[1] Real consumption depended upon real income, both current and lagged a number of periods. However, three different categories of income were identified: (a) wages and salaries, (b) government grants (e.g. pensions), and (c) self-employed income. The lag distributions[2] of each of these were allowed to differ so that, for example, unemployment benefit would be spent more quickly than the profit of the self-employed builder.

The 1977 version of HMT added to these three income terms a distributed lag on the gross liquid assets of the private sector. We shall return to a discussion of this question of a 'real balance effect' in the chapter on Monetarists. But it is safe to record at this stage that the primary motivation for this change was not the pressure of theoretical academic criticism (after all, Zellner, Huang and Chau had established the existence of a liquid assets effect in the US in 1965). Rather, it was caused by the failure of the existing equation to explain the rise in the savings ratio in 1974 and 1975. A rise in the savings ratio implies a fall in the proportion of income consumed. In other words, the existing equation forecast far more consumption than actually happened. Events are the forecasters' cruellest critics.

The 1978 version of HMT contains a radical departure from previous consumption functions. It represents the combined efforts of Davidson et al. (1978) and the staff of the Treasury. There is ample evidence here at least of the speed with which the Treasury has responded to new ideas. The first change is that durable goods expenditure is disaggregated from non-durable consumption. This was always likely to be an improvement since durable goods are lumpy and their purchase is, therefore, more cyclical. Secondly, incomes are treated as homogeneous. Thirdly, unemployment and the price level now play a direct part. Finally, the functional form has a new look about it. It is convenient to write out the two equations with a verbal explanation underneath.

2.1 $$\Delta_4 C = \sum_{i=0}^{3} a_i \ \Delta_4 Y - 109 \ (C-Y)_{t-4}$$

$$- 0.023\Delta \ \Delta_4 UN - 0.919\Delta_4 P$$

The change in real consumers' expenditure on non-durables, C, between the current quarter and the same quarter the previous year (this is the meaning of Δ_4) depends upon (a) current real personal disposable income, Y, and its value for the previous three quarters, (b) real saving four quarters ago, $C - Y$, (c) the *change* in the change in unemployment, UN, between the current quarter and the same quarter the previous year, and (d) the change in the consumers' expenditure price index, P, between the current quarter and the same quarter the previous year. (All variables converted to natural logarithms.)

2.2 $\quad CD = -0.45CD_{t-1} + 0.058Y - 74.5\,\Delta UN$

$$+ 0.007W_{t-1} - 5(r - \dot{P}^c) + J$$

Quarterly consumer durable expenditure, CD, depends upon (a) consumer durable expenditure last period, (b) current personal disposable income, (c) the change in unemployment, (d) personal sector wealth, W, at the end of last period, (e) the difference between the interest rate on consumer loans, r, and the expected rate of increase of consumer prices, $\dot{P}^c$, this is a proxy for the real interest rate, and (f) a variable to capture the effects of changes in hire purchase controls.

Equation 2.1 looks to be the most unconventional. The format by which one takes the change between the same quarter in each year (Δ_4) can, however, be seen as a convenient way of handling the strong seasonal pattern in all the variables. More unusual perhaps are the terms in lagged saving and the price level. These, it is argued, together 'produce an implicit wealth variable', whereas unemployment is included because it picks up an increase in 'precautionary saving' when times are bad. This equation is preferred to previous versions because it is able to explain recent events while the others were not. The consumer durable equation is rather more conventional and needs no further comment.

It should already be clear that the world of the forecaster is a long way from that of the textbooks. Equations 2.1 and 2.2 are the practical counterpart of equation 1.2.

Investment

In most macroeconomic models of the textbook variety investment often plays a critical role. The Keynesian tradition, in particular, gives investment the role of black sheep. It is unforeseen slumps in investment which, through downward multiplier effects, cause depressions. Typically in static models, investment is thought to be either exogenously given or determined by the interest rate. In many dynamic models it depends upon the (expected) rate of change of output. The rationale of this latter relationship is that, since a certain capital stock is required to produce a particular output, any increase in output (at full capacity) requires an increase in the capital stock, i.e. net investment. Gross investment includes that which is necessary to replace existing machines as they wear out.

Investment, for forecasting purposes, is usually disaggregated into many components. Public sector investment is not forecast but is assumed to take place at the levels set out in public expenditure White Papers. HMT separates private investment into (a) manufacturing, (b) private distribution and services, (c) 'other' private investment, and (d) private investment in land and existing buildings. In addition, there is the category of investment that textbooks always ignore — investment in stocks at the manufacturing, wholesale and retail levels. Each of these four categories of investment and three categories of stockbuilding has an equation in HMT. However, it is important to realise that,

> For the two biggest sectors, manufacturing and private distribution and services, which together accounted for over two-thirds of the non-dwelling total in 1976, direct information on investment intentions is available from Department of Industry's surveys and (for manufacturing only) the CBI survey. These sources are thought to be valuable indicators of the immediate future, and short-term forecasts rely heavily on them. The equations for investment in these sectors are therefore primarily of use in simulations and medium-term forecasts. (HMT 1978, p. 2.1)

The equations for each investment category and for each stockbuilding category have a similar structure, so it is sufficient to set out only those for manufacturing investment and manufacturing stockbuilding.

2.3
$$IM_t = RM + 155 + \sum_{i=1}^{12} a_i \, \Delta YM_{t-i} + \sum_{i=2}^{7} b_i CF_{t-i}$$
$$+ \sum_{i=0}^{14} c_i \, \Delta(r_1 - 0.68 \, P^e)_{t-i}$$

> Gross investment in manufacturing industry, IM, is equal to replacement investment, RM, plus (a) a 12-period distributed

lag on the change in industrial output, YM, plus (b) a 7-period distributed lag on the internal cash flow of companies, CF, plus (c) a 14-period distributed lag on the change in the *real* interest rate (i.e., the nominal long-term interest rate, r_1, minus the expected rate of inflation, $\dot{P}^c$).

2.4 $$SM_t = SM_{t-1} + \sum_{i=0}^{7} a_i \, \Delta YM_{t-1} + 0.112 \, \Delta EF_t$$

$$+ \, 0.049 \, \Delta EF_{t-1} + \sum_{i=0}^{4} b_i \, \Delta(r_s - \dot{P}_w)_{t-i}$$

Stocks held in manufacturing industry, SM, equal last period's stocks, plus (a) a 7-period distributed lag on the change in manufacturing output, YM, plus (b) the change in the ratio of actual final sales to forecast final sales, EF, in the current and previous period, plus (c) a 4-period distributed lag on the real interest rate (i.e., the short-term interest rate, r_s, minus the percentage change in the wholesale price index, $\dot{P}_w$).

These two equations have two terms in common. Both the level of investment and the change in stocks held depend upon changes in output for a number of prior periods. They also both have an interest rate term, though in 2.3 it is a real long-term rate and in 2.4 it is a real short-term rate. These in turn differ from the interest rate in 2.2 which was the real interest rate on consumer loans. Another obvious difference between the investment equations and the consumption equations is that investment is subject to longer lags. A change in output takes up to three years to have its full effect on investment and a change in interest rates takes up to three and a half years. Internal cash flow is included in 2.3 because firms find it easier to invest out of profits than to borrow. And the change in ratio of actual final sales to forecast final sales is included to capture the unplanned element of stockbuilding in 2.4.

Exports

The largest category of exports is manufactured goods which are forecast in a single equation. However, exports of ships, aircraft and precious stones are forecast exogenously. The volume of non-manufactured exports excluding oil is related to an index of world industrial production and relative prices. The principal export equation is:

$$2.5 \quad X_t = 8.132 + \sum_{i=0}^{1} a_i \, WT_{t-i} - 0.009t + \sum_{i=0}^{17} b_i \, RC_{t-i}$$

$$+ \sum_{i=0}^{17} c_i RD_{t-i} + \sum_{i=0}^{17} d_i COST_{t-i} \text{(all in logs)}$$

> UK exports of manufactured goods, X, depend upon (a) world trade, WT, in the current and previous period, (b) a negative time trend, t, (c) a 17-quarter distributed lag on (i) the relative competitiveness of UK exports, RC, as compared to other exporting countries, (ii) the relative domestic market price, RD, as compared to export prices, and (iii) the cost of manufactures, $COST$, as compared to export prices.

The term in world trade reflects the fact that exports depend on growing world demand and the time trend 'implies that, if world trade grows at its trend rate, the UK share of its market falls by 4½% a year.' The other three terms reflect UK export prices relative to those of competitors, the attractiveness of exporting as opposed to selling on the home market and, finally, the profitability of exporting. What is most surprising about this equation is that the lags in the last three terms imply that a change in relative prices today will take over four years to have its full effect. Even investment is not subject to such long lags as these.

Imports

HMT contains about nine separate categories of imports, each of which is forecast separately. These are food, drink and tobacco; basic materials; semi-manufactures: manufactured goods; capital goods; other finished manufactures; ships and aircraft; and fuel. It would make things look unnecessarily complicated if each of these were set out, so just two will be used for illustrative purposes, basic materials and manufactured goods.

2.6 $\quad MB_t = 0.8176\ YM_t + 1.664\left(\dfrac{SM_t}{SM_{t-1}}\right) - 0.004474t$

$$+ 2.0521 \qquad \text{(all in logs)}$$

Imports of basic materials, MB, depend upon (a) current manufacturing output, YM, (b) the ratio of manufacturers' stocks of raw materials this period, SM, to that last period, and (c) a negative time trend, t.

2.7 $\quad MM_t = -11.30 + \displaystyle\sum_{i=0}^{5} a_i RELP_{t-i} + \sum_{i=0}^{5} b_i CE_{t-i}$

$$+ 0.0335t + 0.1239\ CAPU_t$$
$$\text{(all in logs)}$$

Imports of manufactures, MM, depend upon (a) a distributed lag on the relative price of imports, $RELP$, as compared to home goods, (b) a distributed lag on consumers' expenditure, CE, on this category of goods, (c) a time trend, t, and (d) an index of capacity utilisation, $CAPU$.

Equation 2.6 reflects the fact that raw materials are imported as an input into a production process. Firms will, therefore, be importing these materials either because they are producing more output or because they are planning to increase their stocks. Equation 2.7 is like a demand equation for a certain category of goods. The demand for imported goods depends upon their relative price and total domestic expenditure on that type of goods. The capacity utilisation term, however, reflects supply factors. If domestic firms are unable to increase supplies there will be an increase in imports.

Invisibles

Most textbook models ignore the existence of invisibles entirely. For economies like the UK, however, they are extremely important and cannot be ignored. 'Invisibles' covers all payments on current account in either direction for which a physical commodity does not cross the international frontier. The most important categories are services, such as insurance or tourism; transfers, such as remittances to relatives abroad;

and interest profits and dividends (IPD) accruing to overseas investments.

The volumes of private services are taken to be demand determined, so UK services bought by foreigners are related to world trade or world industrial production. UK 'imports' of services are related to UK expenditure variables. Relative prices also enter some categories. Transfers are taken to be exogenous as are public sector debits. The IPD elements are forecast by applying interest rates to asset stocks and thus determining actual interest payments. Income from direct investment is determined by world activity and prices on the credit side, and by domestic profits so far as debits are concerned. Again, for illustrative purposes only two equations will be presented here — exports of services other than shipping and travel on the credit side and imports of travel services on the debit side.

2.8 $$XOS = 3.6204 + \sum_{i=0}^{2} a_i WP_{t-i} + \sum_{i=0}^{9} b_i RELW_{t-i}$$

$$+ \ 0.003709t \qquad \text{(all in logs)}$$

Exports of other services, XOS, depend upon (a) world industrial production, WP, (as a proxy for world income), (b) lagged domestic wages relative to foreign consumer prices, $RELW$, and (c) a time trend, t.

2.9 $$MTR = -15.945 + \sum_{i=0}^{6} a_i CS_{t-i} + \sum_{i=0}^{4} b_i RELP_{t-i}$$

$$\text{(all in logs)}$$

Imports of travel services, MTR, depend upon (a) a distributed lag on total consumer expenditure on services, CS, and (b) a distributed lag on domestic retail prices relative to foreign retail prices, $RELP$.

Clearly, the approach to explaining these invisible items is straightforward and unobjectionable. In each case it is merely a matter of finding the relevant expenditure or income category and the appropriate relative price.

Government Expenditure and Taxes

Public sector expenditures are not forecast by means of equations. Rather the forecasters take the published plans for expenditure and treat them as exogenously given. Tax rates are also taken as exogenously determined, but tax revenues are determined by formulae which apply assumed tax rates to the various categories of expenditure and income, which are themselves determined endogenously.

Other Exogenous Factors and the Determination of GDP

We have now outlined the main structure of the model used by HM Treasury to forecast national income or, to be more precise, GDP. It is clear that all that has been done is to assemble the entire set of relationships which combine to determine total domestic expenditures in a manner exactly analogous to Model I of the previous chapter. The only difference is that here the relationships are somewhat disaggregated and it is not possible to make simplifying assumptions about dynamics or about relevant exogenous variables. GDP at factor cost is now determined through two standard identities which are the analogue of equation 1.1:

2.10 $\quad TFE = C + X + IF + IS + CCG + CLA$

> Total final expenditure, *TFE*, equals consumption, *C*, plus exports, *X*, plus gross fixed investment, *IF*, plus total stock-building, *IS*, plus central government consumption, *CCG*, plus local government consumption, *CLA*.

2.11 $\quad Y = TFE - M - A$

> GDP at factor cost, *Y*, equals total final expenditure, *TFE*, less imports, *M*, less the factor cost adjustment, *A* (indirect taxes less subsidies).

There are, however, two important problem areas. The first problem must be handled before the calculation of GDP. The second can be dealt with after the GDP forecast. Firstly, it should be obvious that in order to arrive at a solution for

GDP it is necessary to assign values to a number of variables which are determined outside the system. These include variables such as world trade, world production and competitors' prices as well as domestic variables such as interest rates on financial assets. A view is formed about likely values of these other variables by means of three related but separable forecasting exercises. First, there is what the Treasury calls the World Economic Prospects exercise, or WEP. A new WEP is conducted twice a year, usually before the autumn and spring forecasting rounds. This amounts to taking a view of the likely developments in the world economy based mainly upon a view of the major OECD economies. Second, there is the financial forecast which is constructed in the light of expected interest rate trends and the predicted net financial positions of the main sectors of the economy, viz. the private, corporate, financial and public sectors. Essentially, this exercise takes sectoral balances predicted by the main model — National Income Forecasting Model (NIF) — and generates interest rate predictions. A monetary sector model has been developed at the Treasury which is intended to be integrated with the NIF. A brief outline of this is provided at the end of this chapter. Third, capital flows are examined to forecast the financing requirements of the overall balance of payments in conjunction with the current account equations of the NIF. In principle it can now be used in parallel with the NIF to endogenise the exchange rate. However, in practice it is more normal to assume the path of the exchange rate and thus to forecast reserve changes. Two other minor forecasting exercises are concerned to predict government debt interest payments and supply constraints in particular industries.

The second problem area concerns questions about which the forecaster has to form some view but which are logically consequent upon the basic NIF results. The most interesting and important of these is the question of the level of employment and, thus, also unemployment.

Employment and Unemployment

Employment is separated into three main sectors: (i) manufacturing, (ii) non-trading public sector, and (iii) trading public sector and non-manufacturing private sector. The basic determinant of employment in each sector is the output of each sector. This information is obtained by disaggregating GDP which has already been calculated above. 'Manufacturing output is calculated by taking fixed weight combinations of the relevant components of demand and imports ... the output of the non-trading public sector is measured by expenditure on inputs — the relevant wage and salary bill.' The remaining sector's output is determined as a residual since GDP must equal the sum of sectoral outputs.

Employment in each sector is determined by output in that sector and a time trend. For central and local government it is just a matter of taking the planned expenditure on wages and salaries. Thus:

2.12 $ECG = 0.869 - 0.000586t + 1.0\ CCGE$ (all in logs)

Employment in non-trading central government, ECG, depends upon (a) a negative time trend, t, and (b) the planned level of central government expenditure on wages and salaries, $CCGE$.

The simplicity of this equation derives from the fact that the output is not observed independently of the input. In the manufacturing sector output changes only produce employment changes after a time. So the prediction of employment levels depends not only upon current output but also upon several previous periods.

2.13 $EMF = 6.236 - 0.0015T + \sum_{i=0}^{9} a_i\ YMF_{t-i}$ (all in logs)

Employment in manufacturing industry, EMF, depends upon (a) a time trend, T, reflecting productivity levels, and (b) current and lagged output for 9 previous periods, YMF.

Forecasts of the unemployment rate are now derived by first subtracting total employment from labour supply and then making some allowance for the number of unemployed who actually register. Labour supply is determined exogenously by demographic factors.

Prices and Wages

So far all the variables which have been determined in the above model have been in 'real' terms. That is to say they have been measured in constant price terms. Inflation enters directly only in so far as it distorts real relative prices (say, between exporters and foreign competitors) and real interest rates. The only exception is that the nominal price index enters the equation for non-durable consumers' expenditure. This was first introduced in the 1978 version of the model and represents a radical departure from previous conventions. Hitherto, price indices were required by the Treasury forecasters primarily as 'deflators' for the various expenditure categories to get them all into constant price terms. The forecasting of inflation has for the most part been an exercise which could be carried out independently of the NIF itself. For reasons of space, it is convenient to describe only the short-term forecast method for the retail price index.

'In the short-term, the retail price index is forecast by component, i.e. food, housing including rent, nationalised industries and "other". The first three components are forecast directly using information supplied by other government departments . . .' The 'other' component is forecast using the following equation:

$$2.14 \qquad PRO = TRO + \sum_{i=0}^{8} a_i WI_{t-i} + \sum_{i=0}^{5} b_i MP_{t-i}$$

$$+ \sum_{i=0}^{3} c_i \left(\frac{INDT}{C} \right)_{t-i}$$

Retail price index of 'other' goods, PRO, equals (a) the direct effect of indirect taxes on final goods prices, TRO, plus (b) a distributed lag on trend unit wage costs, WI, in the private sector, plus (c) a distributed lag on the unit value index for imports, MP, other than food, drink and tobacco, plus (d) a distributed lag on the ratio of total indirect taxes, $INDT$ (less rates $\times$ 0.4) to consumers expenditure, C.

The overall retail price index is determined by:

$$2.15 \quad PR = 0.233\,PRF + 0.125\,PRH + 0.075\,PRN$$
$$+\ 0.567\,PRO$$

The retail price index, PR, is a weighted sum of the food price index, PRF, the housing price index, PRH, the nationalised industry price index, PRN, and the 'other' price index, PRO.

The basic 'theory' behind equation 2.14 is in fact an identity. It says that final price per unit output is equal to the sum of wage costs per unit output, material costs per unit output, profit per unit output and indirect taxes per unit output. This relationship must be true by definition, whatever the underlying cause of inflation may be. In addition, however, forecasters typically assume that profits per unit output are constant, and material costs are replaced by import prices. There are two reasons for the latter assumption. One is that a high proportion of raw materials are imported and the other is that many final goods are imported. Indirect taxes appear twice: the first term in equation 2.14 reflects the direct effect of indirect taxes on final goods prices and the last term picks up the indirect effect through intermediate products '. . . on the assumption that businesses do not shift the majority of their rate burden.'

Inflation is, thus, forecast by taking current and past levels of major elements in cost which take time to work their way through to final goods prices. Typically, however, these cost changes have either already happened or are treated as exogenous. Import prices are exogenous so long as the exchange rate is exogenous and during the recent past it has been customary to assume a rate of increase of wages and salaries per head at levels implied by the current incomes policy. However, there is the possibility that wages and salaries could be forecast by means of an 'earnings equation', along the lines of a Phillips curve.

Earnings

The basic earnings equation that is present in HMT for use when a successful incomes policy is not assumed to be in operation is as follows:

2.16 $\quad \Delta AR = \text{Constant} + a_1 \Delta RP - a_2 \Delta RET - a_3 \sum_{i=0}^{1} \ln U$

$$- a_4 \Delta U - a_5 \Delta CYC$$

> The growth in average earnings, AR, depends upon the growth in the retail price index, RP; the change in the proportion of income retained after tax, RET; the log of the level of unemployment, U; the change in employment, ΔU; and a cyclical variable to reflect the seasonal pattern of wage settlements, CYC. (Δ here denotes a ratio of current to previous rather than a difference.)

The unemployment terms are in the tradition of the Phillips curve and the retail price index and retentions ratio appear, as it is assumed that workers will attempt to restore their real disposable income.

Properties of the Model

The only sector of the model that has not been mentioned so far concerns the housing market. There is a sector which first models the flow of funds into building societies and then relates the availability of such funds to house prices and house building activity. Whilst this area is interesting and important in itself, it has not been expanded here because it is not central to the workings of the model. What must now be done is to establish what kind of a model we are dealing with. How does it relate to the textbook models of the previous chapter? Does it have any precise information to give us about things like the multiplier? It might be helpful first to list the equations that have been selected as representative:

- 2.1 Consumption for non-durables
- 2.2 Consumption expenditure on durables
- 2.3 Investment
- 2.4 Stockbuilding
- 2.5 Exports

2.6 Imports of basic materials
2.7 Imports of manufactures
2.8 Exports of services
2.9 Imports of travel services
2.10
2.11 } Total income and expenditure identities
2.12 Employment in central government
2.13 Employment in manufacturing
2.14 Price index of 'other' goods
2.15 Definition of retail price index
2.16 Determination of earnings (for 'incomes policy off' periods)

The core of the model is provided by equations 2.1 to 2.11. This system is exactly analogous to the six equations of Model I except that here the expenditure categories are disaggregated. The equations themselves are, of course, far more complex,largely because they are of necessity dynamic and because there are more exogenous influences. However, the logical structure is exactly the same in so far as national income is demand-determined and aggregate demand consists of the components listed and illustrated in figure 1.1. There are no equations for the monetary sector as in Model II. Interest rates do now have some small influence, but they are determined exogenously, though these omissions will be rectified by the monetary model. The supply side of Model III is not explicitly modelled at all. Supply factors do enter in two obvious places, but this is not central to the national income determination process. First, imports of certain goods depend upon an index of capacity utilisation so that as capacity limits are approached imports are substituted for domestic output. Second, unemployment is forecast on the basis of an assumed labour supply which is equal in effect to the able population of working age. However, both these supply assumptions are entirely arbitrary and do not depend upon economic variables.

It is fortunate that work has recently been published by the forecasters themselves comparing the properties of the three major models in the UK[3]. This work uses the cores of HMT, NI and LBS as they existed in 1977, though augmenting the former two with monetary sectors, which were not in practice fully operative. There are a great many comparisons which can be made and the reader is encouraged to follow these up. For present purposes it is sufficient to compare the simple government expenditure multipliers. The multiplier is defined as the ratio of the change in real GDP to the change in initial expenditure. Obviously, since the models are dynamic, the values of the multipliers will depend upon how many periods are allowed to elapse. The results are obtained by holding all exogenous variables in the model constant (including in this case interest rates, earnings and the exchange rate) and imposing a £100M rise in public authorities final consumption which is subsequently sustained.

> In a symposium on UK models held in 1972, Bispham, using the NI model of 1972/3, reported a real GDP multiplier of 0.98 after eleven quarters with respect to a sustained shock to current government expenditure, while the version of the model reported here gives a multiplier of 0.68 after eleven quarters. Ball, Burns and Miller reported a real multiplier of 1.11 after twenty-four quarters for the 1972 version of LBS model against 1.06 in this simulation. Treasury results with a model of similar vintage reported by Evans and Riley show a real multiplier of 1.33 after sixteen quarters compared to 1.09 in the present version. The lower multiplier values found for the current versions of the NIESR and Treasury models are partly due to the higher import propensities which occur when the estimation period is extended to include more recent experience. (Laury, Lewis and Ormerod 1978, p.56)

What this means is that in the major UK forecasting models of the last decade the value of what is normally called 'the' multiplier has been in the range 0.68 to 1.33 for time periods of the order of three to six years. A central estimate would seem to be a value of 1.0 after about four years. This in itself is an extrodinary result for any model in the Keynesian tradition, as HMT and NI claim to be. The multiplier was after all given the name 'multiplier' because a change in exogenous expenditures was expected to lead to a multiple increase in national income. In Model I with no foreign trade the government expenditure multiplier would equal as a first approximation 1/m.p.s., where m.p.s. is the marginal propensity to save. A reasonable value to assume for the marginal propensity to save might be 0.2, so the multiplier would be 5.0. The forecasting models have lower multipliers because they have other leakages as well as saving — notably imports and taxes. But they do not typically have endogenous negative feedbacks from the monetary sector as in Model II and they do not have aggregate supply constraints or price level feedbacks as in Model III. If the multiplier calculations were to incorporate such features they would result in even smaller values than those reported above. We shall postpone a discussion of the significance of these results until Chapter 9 on crowding out.

Post Script: The Treasury Monetary Model

At the time of writing, versions of the Treasury Monetary and Capital Flows models have just been published for the first time (see Spencer and Mowl 1978 and Lomax and Denham 1978). The treatment of capital flows is not central to our theme and so these will not be discussed. However, it may be helpful to provide a brief description of the monetary model, though we should bear in mind the warning that 'The models described are still at the stage of research. They are sufficiently advanced to contribute to forecasting and analysis, but there is still much work to be done before we shall feel able to use them without great caution.' (Spencer and Mowl 1978, Foreword.)

The important thing to notice right away about the Treasury Monetary Model is that it is not primarily based upon the demand and supply of money as is the monetary sector of the IS–LM model. Rather it is structured around the portfolio behaviour of six sectors of the economy: the public sector; the commercial banks; the Bank of England Banking Department and National Giro; discount houses, the non-bank private sector; and the overseas sector. Between these six sectors 13 different categories of financial assets and liabilities are identified. The main focus of the model is, by specifying the demands and supplies by each sector for various assets and liabilities, to determine how the various interest rates will be linked. In this way, for example, it becomes possible to analyse the chain reaction through various financial markets of, say, a government bond issue or a deliberate change in minimum lending rate.

In common with the IS—LM model the portfolio behaviour of the private sector of the economy is largely separable from real expenditure decisions. An excess supply of one asset is reflected in an excess demand for another, and not as an excess demand for goods. However, in contrast to the IS—LM model, the saving, or financial surplus, is taken as an exogenous input into the Monetary Model and this determines private sector demands for additional financial assets in each period. In this way the outcome determined in the National Income Forecasting Model (NIF) outlined above feeds into the Monetary Model (MM). The principal feedback from the MM to the NIF seems to be in the form of interest rate effects, though there is an obvious potential for the addition of credit rationing and other possible direct 'liquid asset' effects if so desired.

The other important option opened up by the existence of a complete model which incorporates the NIF, the MM and capital flows is that of endogenising the exchange rate. It has always been standard practice when operating the NIF alone to assume that the exchange rate follows some particular path. Once a model is available which incorporates the entire balance of payments, including asset flows, it then becomes possible to simulate a floating exchange rate and follow through its implications via inflation and interest rates to the whole economy.

The properties of this and other forecasting models will obviously require many books and articles to be written before they are fully understood. It is to be hoped that this chapter will stimulate students to pursue an interest in this area.

Notes

1. See Evans (1969), chapter 2, for an outline of tests of the permanent income hypothesis.
2. The term 'lag distributions' or 'distributed lags' refers to the coefficients or weights attached to a succession of lagged explanatory variables.
3. See Laury, Lewis and Ormerod (1978).

PART II
Factions

In the following four chapters we begin our discussion of controversies. The main controversy of the last decade or so has been between Monetarists and Keynesians. It is impossible to define either of these terms without losing much of the flavour of the debate. So the approach adopted here is to give some idea of the broad viewpoint of various ill-defined groups. This will prepare the ground for a discussion of more specific issues in Part III. Many of the important distinctions between groups will emerge later rather than sooner.

3

Non Protagonists: Anti or Eclectic

Philosophy, that lean'd on Heaven before,
Shrinks to her second cause, and is no more.
Physic of Metaphysic begs defence,
And Metaphysic calls for aid on sense!
See Mystery to Mathematics fly!
In vain! they gaze, turn giddy, rave and die.
ALEXANDER POPE

This chapter serves as a reminder that the majority of economists would not fit easily into any of the factions caricatured in the following three chapters. Its aim is to provide the student with a guide to the many other attitudes that he will encounter towards the analysis of these central economic issues. Most economists tend to inherit the approach to the subject of their own teachers. Only rare men of vision have the courage to make a clean break from existing conventions of thought in the face of pressure to conform from their colleagues and mentors. Where you start out in economics very much determines where you will end up.

The remainder of the economics profession will be characterised as consisting of a number of discrete groups. These should be thought of as attitudes rather than individuals since any individual may subscribe to partial membership of more than one group.

Theoretical Purists

A very influential group of economists, especially influential in the UK, devote themselves to what might be called 'high theory'. Many of them are mathematicians by training and they proceed by the application of mathematics to economic models. In order to facilitate their methodology, the models built are typically of a high degree of abstraction, often being constructed on the basis of assumptions which are well known to be extremely unrealistic.

The attraction of this *modus operandi* is that it is intellectually rigorous. Any deduction arrived at by the correct application of mathematics is valid and cannot be questioned on the basis of its internal logic. Only if the entire conceptual experiment is uninteresting can the work be faulted and it will usually not be so criticised by other members of the group. The other attraction of 'high theory' is that it requires no knowledge of, or feeling for, the working of a real economy. Logical consistency is the criterion of value, not realism. There is usually no possibility of testing the models developed.

To the theoretical purist, macroeconomics as currently conducted is a waste of time. It involves unjustified aggregation. Many of the variables and indices are extremely arbitrary. Most of the relationships used to build macro-models are merely assertions which have little or no grounding in (high) theory. It is, therefore, easy to think of reasons why these relationships might not hold and so, even if they describe the data fairly well, there is no reason to accept them as valid. Controversies, such as those discussed in this book, are of no real substance since all positions rely upon simplifications which cannot be justified from first principles.

The economics profession needs to have theoretical purists, but it cannot live by them alone. If there is a payoff to 'high theory' it is in the long run. In the meanwhile economists will be called upon to give advice on current issues. High theory is an investment for the future; others in the profession would prefer to provide output for current consumption.

Statistical Purists

The intellectual status of the statistical or econometric theorist is second only to that of the theoretical purist. Members of this group are primarily concerned with the theory of estimation and of hypothesis testing. If economic theory (or even common sense!) leads us to expect that a particular relationship will exist between two or more variables, how should we test for the existence of this particular relationship? What is the epistemological status of the result obtained? With what degree of confidence can we believe that the data are consistent with the existence of the hypothetical relationship?

The theoretical econometrician, like the high theorist, typically proceeds by the means of analysing the properties of mathematical models. In this case, however, the goal of model building is not primarily to develop equations which characterise relationships between economic variables. Rather the aim is to draw inferences for appropriate estimation techniques from some assumptions about the statistical process which generates the data. For example, the classical linear model which is the theoretical basis for ordinary least squares estimation is built on the assumption of a random disturbance which is normally distributed with a zero mean and a constant variance. The econometrician would be concerned to know what happens if these assumptions were untrue. What now would be an appropriate estimation technique?

The general problem with all empirical work is that one is attempting to test statements about how the world works by reference to a small part of world experience. In statistical terminology one is trying to infer properties of a total population from a small sample of that population. The theoretical econometrician, who has been trained to look for difficulties in the inference procedure, naturally regards most of the empirical results presented by macroeconomists with the greatest scepticism. There are two reasons for this. The first is that econometricians look at *all* empirical work with suspicion. Job security requires that estimation cannot be a simple procedure. The second reason is that the typical macroeconomist is not himself an econometrician and so will not be quite up to date with the latest estimation techniques or *au fait* with what aspect of estimation problems is causing current concern.

The econometrician should be in a position to settle controversies. However, no major controversy in macroeconomics has ever been settled by an econometrician setting up two or more mutually exclusive rival hypotheses and eliminating all but one by resort to the data. A more likely outcome would be either that all rival hypotheses are rejected or that at least two cannot be rejected. Even more likely, however, (see the final chapter) is that parties to a controversy will be unable to agree on *exactly* what the key issue in the controversy is. Thus macroeconomists will have to learn to live with high theorists and econometricians looking down on them, as indeed the latter two will have to learn that they need the former — to pay the rent!

Eclectics

An eclectic has an open mind on the issues and takes in the best ideas from whatever source they come. The true eclectic would not admit to being a member of any single school of thought. By far the largest number of economists would, presumably, regard themselves as falling into this group. However, human capital, like capital in the theory of the firm, is flexible in the long run but fixed in the short run. In the long run we are all eclectic, but in the short run most would approach any given issue in terms of one of the existing approaches. For the most part, then, the price that is paid for preserving a position of eclecticism is silence. Eclectics are the group who have not said enough to warrant a classification by their peers.

This section will obviously have to be short because this group has no position to explain. The attraction of belonging to this group is obvious — one can attack everybody without ever being subject to criticism oneself. Yet surely progress in a discipline has never been made by those who sit on a fence. The important thing is not to be seen never to make a mistake, but rather to be prepared to admit a mistake when the evidence points to one.

Radicals or Marxists

One point of view which every student should familiarise himself with is that of the radical economist. Every economist should have some broader view of why he proceeds as he does. The radical critique of modern economics is so fundamental that a full appreciation of it should force upon the student a justification of his own methodology. A convenient collection of papers in the radical tradition in the UK can be found in Green and Nore (1977).

Modern economics is bourgeois economics. It is constructed around a value system which is false — the value system of one class in society which should not be accepted as universal. Microeconomics is built upon the myth that every actor is a free agent whose rational pursuit of self interest leads to the common good. In reality one group in society inherits a position in the structure of power and wealth which enables it to exploit the other group to its own advantage. Macroeconomics is an exercise in social engineering designed to make the working classes accept policies which are not in their interest.

The fundamental issue for the radical economist is the distribution of income and wealth between classes. This question is inevitably viewed through the Marxist dichotomy of capitalists and workers. See, for example, Beutal (1977):

> ... We suggest that the most significant 'clustering' of inequalities arises from the position in the process of production ... Every system of production includes a specific set of social relationships. Where surplus production occurs and is appropriated by a minority, the division of labour is exploitative and class relationships emerge. The main class division is a dichotomous one between those who own the means of production and those who have no private property rights in the means of production.
>
> In capitalist society the relationship between the bourgeoisie and the proletariat is necessarily antagonistic. This can be explained, at a simple level, by pointing out that wages are a cost to the capitalist but a source of livelihood to the worker ... Every dominant group will represent their interests as the common interest of all the members of society ...
>
> For a proper understanding of these patterns we need to base our analysis of inequalities on the concept of class which is grounded in the relations of production.

The economics profession by implication are the lackeys of the capitalist class. They are paid to preserve the status quo. Radical economists by contrast are people of vision who have penetrated the facade and are able to point out the 'inherent contradiction of the capitalist system' from a more or less neutral point of view. Or, at least, they frame their arguments in terms of the values of the working class who would otherwise go unrepresented.

The problem with radical economics is that it has a point. It is certainly true that many economists are motivated by making capitalism work more efficiently. Few of them would apologise for that. It is also true that all economists let their values dictate their approach to issues and indeed the issues chosen. There is no way of avoiding that so long as human beings are involved. What radical economists really object to is the use of other people's values rather than their own. Every problem for the radical economist is forced into the harness of class conflict. Thus Harris (1977) approaches balance of payments policy as follows:

> . . . Since the nation consists of antagonistic classes which each have their own irreconcilable interests, there can be no such thing as 'the national interest'. It follows that the state cannot in fact represent the national interest (although individual state employees and politicians may think they are trying to) and must therefore represent the interests of particular classes. Under capitalism, the state represents in a general sense the interests of capitalists (who retain control of economic activity) and it takes measures with respect to the balance of payments only to the extent that this is necessary in the interests of capital (or of particular blocks of capital) rather than taking measures in 'the national interest'. For example, in the case of Britain, it has been in the interests of the dominant block of the capitalist class to expand its operations abroad (that is to carry out foreign investment). In consequence, Britain's long-term capital account has been in chronic deficit, but the British state's response to the overall balance of payments deficit which results has without exception been to bring in measures to cut back workers' living standards and thereby assist the current account to offset this capital outflow (and this has more direct effects which assist capitalists in their operation of capital in Britain). (p.127)

This analysis could, in principle, be correct: however, it is hard to believe that the last sentence in particular could be further from the truth. For example, in every year since 1972 there has been a considerable surplus on the net private long-term capital account of the balance of payments and there is certainly no evidence of a 'chronic deficit' before that. Indeed, it would be surprising if there were, because the UK has had very strict controls on overseas investments since the Second World War. The first sign of a relaxation of these controls came in the June 1979 Budget because the pound was *too strong* (i.e. bad for industrial employment). Indeed, any inspection of the balance of payments accounts makes it obvious that UK balance of payments problems are situated in the trade account, i.e. are associated with an excess of domestic absorption over output. If anything, capital *inflows* and interest from abroad have helped maintain domestic consumption above what it would otherwise have been.

No doubt the radical economist will have an alternative story to explain these data, but that is not the point. The point is that the radical economist makes an act of faith just as any economist. The worrying thing is that radical economics to date, in the UK, has been too jingoistic and doctrinaire, even more so than economics as a whole. Its protagonists have done little more than provide an umbrella for the shelter of those who find modern economics too difficult.[1] The economics profession would be wiser for a serious radical critique, but this will not come unless the radicals are prepared to sacrifice outdated dogma in favour of increased rigour. The leading radical economist to date is still Karl Marx. He would surely not write the same book today.

Institutional Descriptivists

The faint hearted who feel uncomfortable with theoretical generalities and models of causation have at hand an alternative method of proceeding. This method must in some degree be present if economics is going to explain the 'real world' but there are many who pursue it as an end in itself. The method may be called descriptivism. It involves, not the search for general principles of behaviour, but rather the exposition of mere information about how things are.

Subscribers to this methodology are usually motivated by a disbelief in the existence of behavioural regularities and are instead driven by an often implicit belief that if enough information is provided about a phenomenon its explanation will become self-evident. The existence of data and understanding of institutions is, of course, important but they will never be adequate on their own to provide answers to the simple questions: Why? and What Next? For these we must continue to search for common patterns which will form the basis of our understanding.

Note

1. The only possible exception to this criticism in the UK is the neo-Ricardian literature associated with the re-switching controversy and stimulated by Sraffa (1960), though it is not clear to what extent this literature should be called 'radical' as opposed to 'high theory.'

4
Keynesians

*To tax and to please, no more than to love and to be
wise, is not given to men.*
BURKE

Keynesian economics was the orthodoxy for certainly two
decades after the Second World War and continues to be the
dominant corpus of macroeconomic thought in the UK at
present. In the United States, however, it is fair to say that
by 1969 when even President Nixon endorsed the famous
dictum 'We are all Keynesians now', the evolution of the basic
model had progressed to such an extent (particularly in
response to the monetarist critique) that many British
Keynesians would not have endorsed it. There is absolutely
no benefit to be obtained from engaging in the semantic
exercise of defining the term 'Keynesian' (or indeed 'money'),
but it is important to be clear what kind of view of the
economy and of economic policy people have in mind when
they use the term. It is now quite commonplace in the British
press to see statements such as the following:

> The extent of the retreat from the traditional Keynesian style of
> economic management, under this Government, could hardly have
> been made more clear than by the events of the past ten days.
> Minimum lending rate at 12½% and bank loans to top companies
> costing a record 5½% in real terms, combined with an officially
> expected slowdown in the economy, carries a very clear and simple
> message: the growth rate is now virtually the last thing the Chan-
> cellor takes into account when framing new policies. (*Sunday
> Times*, 19 November 1978, p. 63).

The purpose of this chapter is first to explain what is normally understood by 'the traditional Keynesian style of economic management' and second to provide a brief introduction to some recent developments in macroeconomics. These have come about as a result of attempts to reinterpret the economics of Keynes, as distinct from the model which was distilled from Keynes' writing by his early followers. It is this latter which we now refer to as 'Keynesian'. Many of the UK Cambridge 'old guard' never accepted the 'Keynesian' interpretation of Keynes. This interpretation was largely due to Hansen (1953), though it came to form the basis of the conventional wisdom in the UK.

The Keynesian Revolution and Keynesian Cases

The Keynesian model of how the economy works can either be thought of as Model I in its entirety or as special cases of Models II and III. It is convenient to discuss each of these in turn before discussing what the appellation 'Keynesian' normally means in policy discussions, though it is worth pointing out at the outset that the 'Keynesian' model was basically a closed economy model. This made its applicability to Britain doubtful from the start except in very special circumstances.

Consider the simplest possible version of Model I for an economy which has no imports or exports. There are just two equations — the national income accounting identity and the consumption function. Government expenditure and investment are exogenously given.

4.1 $\quad Y \equiv C + I + G$

4.2 $\quad C = \alpha + \beta Y$

4.3 $\quad G = G_0$

4.4 $\quad I = I_0$

All the variables are in real terms and all are *flows* of expenditure or income per period. It is presumed that there are unemployed resources, so that a change in the exogenous expenditures will produce an increase in real output and, therefore, of real income. The 'solution' to the model is obtained by substituting for C, G and I into 4.1 and solving for Y. Thus

4.5 $$Y = \frac{\alpha + I_0 + G_0}{1 - \beta}$$

The coefficient on the exogenous expenditures, $1/(1-\beta)$, tells us how much income will change for any change in exogenous expenditures and is often known as 'the multiplier'. It is called this because if the coefficient β were to be of the order of 0.8, which is not unreasonable, then $1/(1-\beta)$ would be 5, i.e. a change in exogenous expenditures would produce a change in income five times greater.

The diagram used to explain Model I is familiar as figure 4.1. There is some level of national income at which all resources are fully employed, $\bar{Y}$. The principal message of the Keynesian revolution is that if aggregate expenditures are insufficient then the system will settle into an equilibrium (at least for a

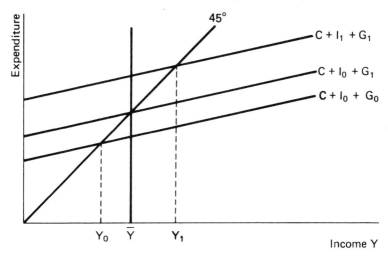

Figure 4.1

significant period) where resources are less than fully employed. The classical system, in contrast, was thought to
work in such a way that prices adjusted up or down to clear
all markets according to whether there was excess demand or
supply. If investment and government expenditure are at
levels $I_0 G_0$, then national income will be Y_0. At this level
there is unemployment because the full employment level of
national income is higher. There will be no tendency for this
unemployment to disappear within the time horizon of the
analysis. The major policy significance of this analysis, however,
is that there is a simple solution to the problem.

The cause of this unemployment is a deficiency of aggregate
expenditures. It can be eliminated if the government is prepared to increase its net injection of expenditures into the
system. This means that the government should deliberately
spend more in the economy than it is raising in taxes. In other
words, it should run a budget deficit. Previously, of course,
the annual budget was simply a way of raising the right
revenue to finance government expenditure. Keynesian
economics is an intellectual justification for the use of the
budget as the major tool for regulating the level of economic
activity.

Model I is often referred to as the income—expenditure
system or simply the expenditure system, as in Chapter 1.
There can be no doubt at all that the formalisation of the
analysis of effective demand failure which it presents was a
fundamental breakthrough in economics. Economists of nearly
all persuasions have added it to their analytical toolbox and
would not question its relevance to the problem it was aimed
at, i.e. deep and sustained depression. However, it would be
foolish to claim that the apparatus is adequate to analyse
other economic problems which have a different origin. For
example, what if expenditures exceed full-employment real
income at $C + I_1 + G_1$? Here it is common to refer to the
existence of an inflationary gap (equal to $I_1 - I_0$). But inflation
itself cannot remove this gap since all variables are in real
terms. The model is incomplete. Macroeconomics today is
still about what has been left out. Keynesians emphasise
what was right with the model; Monetarists (and others)
emphasise what was omitted.

The expenditure system is certainly not the model of Keynes' 'General Theory'. This is more usually, though perhaps incorrectly, interpreted as being the money-augmented expenditure system or IS—LM model. This is Model II of Chapter 1. The only additions are relationships for the demand and supply of money and a link from money interest rates to investment expenditures. The Keynesian message above can be shown in an exactly analogous way. Figure 4.2(a),

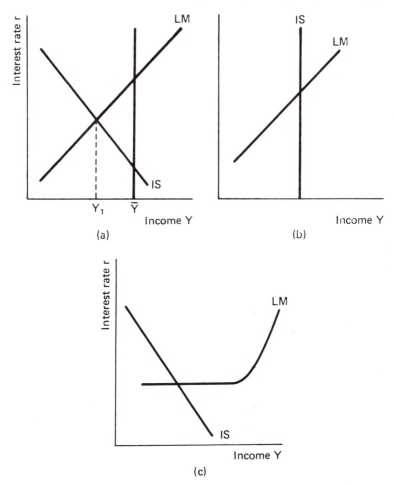

(a)

(b)

(c)

Figure 4.2

for example, shows an equilibrium for the system at less than full-employment real income, $\bar{Y}$. Again the unemployment can be eliminated by an increase in the budget deficit, thus shifting the IS curve to the right. However, in that diagram the same result (with respect to income) could be achieved by increasing the money stock, thereby shifting LM to the right.

The numerical properties of Models I and II are not identical, however. It has already been seen that the multiplier is smaller in II than I because there is negative feedback from the monetary sector. Higher income increases demand for money which raises interest rates, for a given money stock. Keynesians have justified ignoring the monetary sector by the appropriate use of two specific assumptions, though neither is necessary to an understanding of the views of Keynes himself. Indeed, neither is contained in the 'General Theory'. The first of these is that investment is inelastic with respect to the rate of interest (figure 4.2(b)). If this were true, Model I could tell us all we need to know about the real economy. Money supply affects interest rates but interest rates do not affect any real behaviour. The simple multiplier is now appropriate. The second assumption is that there is a liquidity trap so that the LM curve is horizontal (figure 4.2(c)). This means that changes in the money stock get 'hoarded' and do not influence interest rates so there are no real effects even if investment is interest-elastic. This is the famous case of 'pushing on a string'.

While the latter assumption was used to justify Model I in its early days, British Keynesians increasingly defended their position, in the 1950s and 1960s, by reference to the former. The most influential empirical support for this view of investment behaviour was a survey of 37 businessmen reported by Meade and Andrews (1951), most of whom claimed that the interest rate did not influence their investment decisions. The same survey could in fact be used to sustain the opposite conclusion, since a small number of firms admitted that they were affected, which may amount to a significant effect in the aggregate. Nonetheless, it has to be admitted that at least until recently it has proved extremely difficult to establish an interest rate effect on investment in the UK, though this may be due more to the former policy of pegging interest rates than to investment behaviour itself. A survey of the evidence in this area is provided by Savage (1978) and a study which finds significant interest effects is Hines and Catephores (1970). There is a special case of Model III which is often called Keynesian. Again it does not appear in Keynes' 'General Theory' but has entered popular discussion as if it did, following Modigliani (1944). This relies upon the assumption that, while there is no general money illusion, money wages are inflexible in a downward direction. If it is assumed that there is an initial equilibrium at full employment, then the aggregate supply curve is vertical above the equilibrium but sloped below the equilibrium, as in figure 4.3. In effect, the assumption of downward inflexibility of money wages means that there is money illusion in a downward but not an upward direction. A fall in aggregate demand from AD_0 to AD_1 produces a fall in prices. But, because money wages do not fall, the real wage rises. At a higher real wage firms employ less labour and, with a given capital stock, produce less output. So national income falls from $\bar{Y}$ to Y_1. Employment will remain at this new low level unless there is a reduction in

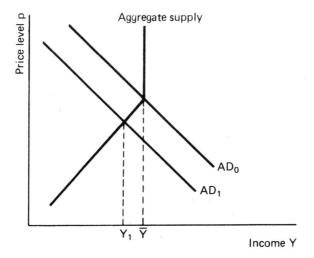

Figure 4.3

money wages or an increase in aggregate demand. Above the full-employment level of output an increase in aggregate demand will increase the price level but not the level of real income. We shall see below that, while the case of real wages being too high is not essential for the existence of 'Keynesian' unemployment, it could form the basis of what is now known as 'classical' unemployment.

Keynesian Economic Management

It is clear that macroeconomic management in the UK during the 1950s and 1960s was governed by Keynesian principles. The exchange rate was fixed, so the domestic inflation rate was clearly related to the world rate which was in turn very low. Economic policy was largely a tightrope walk with unemployment on one side and balance of payments deficits on the other. If the balance of payments was in crisis, as judged by the official reserves, the economy would be deflated. As a result unemployment would rise, so reflation would be undertaken as soon as the reserve position seemed satisfactory. This pattern entered common parlance as the 'stop-go' cycle.

The economic instrument which adopted the centre of the stage was undoubtedly the budget, i.e. fiscal policy. Budgets were (and still are) normally annual events occurring in April, though it became quite commonplace to have 'mini budgets' in July or November. The experience of the time appeared to be that slightly excessive expansion ('overheating') would be associated with lower unemployment but slightly higher inflation and a deteriorating balance of payments. Overheating would be halted by a budget which raised taxes or reduced government expenditure. Slack would be taken up by the reverse.

Monetary policy was not non-existent, but it was largely a residual determined by either the necessity to finance the government borrowing requirement or by the imperatives of the external balance. The money stock was definitely not a target. If anything was a target it was the level of interest rates. In normal times the aim of the Bank of England would be to maintain an 'orderly market' for government debt. Any run on foreign exchange reserves would be countered, however, by a sharp upward rise in Bank Rate, now known as Minimum Lending Rate. Monetary policy was thus constrained by the fiscal stance of the Treasury and by the commitment to a fixed exchange rate. It is now more fully realised how these two factors severely delimit the possibilities of independent monetary policy, particularly when international capital is highly mobile. Inconsistencies which arose in the 1960s were increasingly resolved by imposing quantitative ceilings on bank lending. These remained until they were swept away by the ill-fated reforms known as 'Competition and Credit Control' which were introduced in September 1971.

This concentration upon fiscal policy probably explains why (in conjunction with the special assumptions mentioned above) the major forecasting models in the UK have been built largely as expenditure systems. Indeed, analysis which focuses upon expenditure changes leading through multipliers to income changes is the core of what most economists think of as Keynesian analysis. Chapter 10 on fine tuning will clarify 'the retreat' from Keynesian policies. However, a few points can be anticipated at this stage.

It is very important not to underestimate the importance of the external environment for an open economy like the UK. During the 1950s and early 1960s there was a steady growth in world trade and virtually no inflation in world prices. However, during the late 1960s world inflation began to accelerate, culminating in the commodity price boom and oil price rise in 1973. This has been attributed by some to US policies in financing the Vietnam War and by others to a series of coincidences. If the UK had retained a fairly restrictive policy during this period the economy would probably have benefited from export-led growth. However, the excessive domestic stimulation associated with the policies of Mr Barber, accompanied by currency depreciation, guaranteed that the internal inflationary experience would be worse than that abroad, as indeed the 1967 devaluation had led to a deterioration of domestic inflation. For a time after the 1973 boom burst, unemployment was seen to rise while inflation was also rising, and unemployment had also been rising in 1968 and

1969. So the economic environment which had come to evidence 'stagflation' suddenly appeared inconsistent with the Keynesian or 'fiscalist' model. Small wonder that previous policies had to be re-examined.

The Keynesian Riposte

In the USA the conventional wisdom about the appropriate macroeconomic model evolved from the simple expenditure system, largely in response to the monetarist critique and the inflationary experience which made the critique necessary. There has remained to this day in the UK a group of 'extreme Keynesians' who appear to have taken up even more entrenched positions rather than admit that their model may be improved by adding monetary variables. Their uniting factor is this opposition to Monetarism rather than any coherent interpretation of 'pure' Keynesian economics. The particular forte of this group is thinking up people other than British Chancellors (and their economic advisers!) to blame for UK inflation. Lord Kahn (1976), for example, believes that: 'The international wage explosion can be traced back to the Netherlands, as a result, because of the entry in 1959 of the Liberal party into the coalition government, of the breakdown in the Dutch statutory prices and incomes policy . . .' One of the main reasons for UK inflation being worse than abroad, according to Kahn, is that, 'Our central employer (CBI) and trade union (TUC) organisations are very feeble bodies and the men who run them are sadly lacking in intelligence.'

We shall return to this issue in the chapter on inflation. However, it is worth noting at this stage that the reason for the emergence of these strange *ad hoc* stories about inflation is that, in so far as there is an explicit model, it is entirely in real terms. In other words, *since nominal wages and prices are exogenous to the Keynesian model, any story will do.* Trade unions, the Arabs, moral decline, the student uprising, in fact any event which precedes the bout of inflation you are trying to explain will suffice as an explanation. Surely an explicit model of inflation is preferable if one can be found.

Another illustration of how the extreme Keynesians either

misunderstood or ignored monetary factors is offered by Eltis (1976). He points to the evidence submitted by Sir Roy Harrod, Lord Kaldor and Lord Kahn to the Radcliffe Committee. Harrod proposes a major increase in the money supply so that '. . . the long term rate of interest would come down to 3 per cent quite naturally without any fuss or bother.' Kaldor offered advice on 'The Dangers of a Regime of Stable Prices' and Kahn was of the opinion that 'To my mind the [government's] overall deficit is of no significance.' Small wonder the UK has had one of the worst growth and inflation records in the Western World since that period.

There is, however, a more serious Keynesian riposte to monetarism which deserves consideration. In the UK it is associated with the Radcliffe Report itself, the American parallel being the work of Gurley and Shaw. In the words of the Radcliffe Report:

> . . . The factor which monetary policy should seek to influence or control is something that reaches beyond what is known as the 'supply of money'. It is nothing less than the state of liquidity of the whole economy . . .
> . . . We have found it impossible to treat any one group of institutions as exclusively important in this connection or even as so important in comparison with the others as to excuse the latter from consideration. (para. 981)

This view is perfectly coherent but it led many anti-monetarists to offer the criticism that 'money' could not be defined in any meaningful way. The question of the appropriate level of aggregation of behavioural relations is not one from which Keynesians themselves should be immune. However, the serious question which Radcliffe poses is a fundamental one for the sustenance of monetarism. It is this: for *any* reasonable definition of money, is the elasticity of substitution between money and its closest substitute sufficiently small and stable as to substantiate the distinction? The vast weight of evidence seems to suggest that the answer is an emphatic yes. There are really two separate aspects to this problem so far as policy is concerned. The first is about the stability of the demand for money function and the second is whether the authorities can control the money stock. At one time it would have been possible to identify a Monetarist by whether or not he sub-

scribed to the following two propositions. Firstly, for whatever definition of money is chosen, it does appear possible to
estimate a stable demand function. Secondly, it does seem
possible for the authorities to control 'the money stock' with
the desired effects upon economic behaviour in a floating
exchange rate situation. However, as we shall see below, such
a test would no longer be adequate.

Keynes Resurrected

It may be no coincidence that decline in the regard for the
simple Keynesian model has been accompanied by a theoretical
reappraisal of 'what Keynes really meant.' This has stimulated
an upsurge in macreconomic theory in what is now thought
to be the tradition of Keynes. However, by splitting the
Keynesians off from Keynes it has made them even more
exposed to criticism than they were before. After the Reforma-
tion came the Inquisition.

The prime movers in the reappraisal of Keynes were Robert
Clower (1965) and Axel Leijonhufvud (1968). Leijonhufvud's
book was particularly important, partly in its own right but
partly also because it explained to the economics profession
some of the things Clower has been saying for some time.
Leijonhufvud asks himself, 'How can it be that a deep depression associated with the greatest monetary collapse of all time
leads to the story that money does not matter?' He concludes
that:

> To the extent that preference for the use of fiscal measures for
> stabilisation purposes rests on the belief that they will have an
> amplified impact on aggregate demand, we do not find a case for
> them along the lines of analysis pursued here as far as states of the
> system 'fairly close' to full employment are concerned.
>   By pursuing Keynes' analysis we have ended up with an essentially
> 'monetary' view of Great Depressions. In a very general sense, at
> least, quantity theorists and Keynesians should be able to agree on
> one thing — how great disasters are fashioned. On one view or the
> other, the system becomes prone to them only when it has first been
> squeezed dry of 'liquidity'. (Leijonhufvud, 1969)

This new wave of Keynesian economics will no doubt merit

many books and articles in its own right. The most that can be offered here is a very brief introduction.

The classical (Walrasian) model of a market economy was hypothesised to work by means of an imaginary 'auctioneer.' Transactors entered the market at the beginning of each 'week' with a set of goods and services on offer (supplies) and a set of demands which they would communicate to the auctioneer. There would then be an adjustment process (tatônnement), starting from some initial price vector, such that the prices of goods that were in excess demand would rise and the prices of goods in excess supply would fall. Trade would take place only when prices had been found which cleared the markets, i.e. equilibrium prices. In this way there could never be an excess supply in equilibrium (e.g. unemployment) because prices would adjust until it was eliminated. This is basically a barter economy since goods would now be exchanged for goods. Every offer of a good is simultaneously a demand for another, so Walras' Law (that the sum of excess demands and supplies is zero) must always hold.

One of Clower's contributions is to point out that in an actual monetary economy Walras' Law need not hold. Suppose an initial price vector exists such that some labour is unemployed. Workers have a supply of labour and a demand for goods. However, the demand for goods cannot be expressd in the market until after workers have received money for their labour. Firms are not going to hire labour until they see the money going down for the goods. It is Catch 22. The actual excess supply of labour is matched by a notional demand for goods, but, the *effective* demand for goods is deficient, so the workers do not get employed and the goods do not get produced.

What is shown here is that the existence of unemployment does not necessarily imply that the real wage is too high but rather that the whole price mechanism is at fault. False signals are being transmitted and there is no tendency for these signals to be quickly corrected. Prices themselves are relatively sticky so it is the quantities of employment and trade which have to suffer, but there is no presumption as to which prices are wrong so the mere reduction of money wages will not guarantee full employment.

The existence of money balances is vital to the behaviour of the system because they provide a buffer stock which insulates the economy against disturbances. Let us suppose that there is an exogenous fall in effective demand. Firms lose sales so they lay off workers. In Keynes' multiplier process the laid off workers cut spending, so more workers are laid off. The initial disturbance is amplified. However, this will only happen when the unemployed have been drained of their buffer stock of liquidity (i.e. in a depression following a monetary collapse). Otherwise the initially unemployed worker will, at least temporarily, maintain his effective demand by living off his buffer stock (his savings) and thereby cut the multiplier process short in its tracks — there will be no second round effect. Hence the conclusion of Leijonhufvud quoted above.

This reappraisal of Keynes has led in two related directions. First there is the temporary equilibrium literature which is beyond our scope to discuss, but second there is a rich and growing literature on constrained equilibrium macroeconomic models. The primary contributors to this literature have been Barro and Grossman (1976) and Malinvaud (1977).

Malinvaud develops a simple model in which there is a single goods market, a labour market and a stock of nominal money in existence. Nominal prices and wages are fixed. Analysis concerns the range of possible outcomes. There are two markets, each of which may show excess demand or supply, so there are four apparent cases. When suppliers are offering more than is demanded in both markets because of

		Goods market	
		Excess supply	Excess demand
Labour market	Excess supply	Keynesian unemployment	Classical unemployment
	Excess demand	/////////	Repressed inflation

Figure 4.4

lack of effective demand, there is Keynesian unemployment (figure 4.4). If firms can sell all they produce but labour is unemployed, this is classical unemployment. The third case has excess demand in both markets, in which case, because prices are rigid, there is repressed inflation. The fourth case would have firms unable to sell all their output but at the same time demanding more labour than they can hire. This is ruled out as being inconsistent with rational behaviour on the part of firms, as they would not hire more workers if they could not sell even current output. So only three substantive cases remain.

These three areas of disequilibrium can be plotted in money wage/money price space (figure 4.5). Recall that there is a given stock of nominal assets, M_0, and that whatever the prices happen to be they are not flexible. There is one combination of wages and prices which represents the Walrasian full-employment equilibrium, W.

Roughly speaking, we may say that Keynesian unemployment occurs when prices are too high in comparison with the nominal assets M_0 of consumers and given the volume of autonomous demand g. Classical unemployment, on the other hand, is typical of a situation in which real wages are too high, so that firms do not find it profitable to employ all their labour force. Repressed inflation occurs when

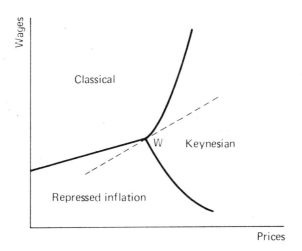

Figure 4.5

both prices and wages are so low that individual assets have a large amount of purchasing power, and when people choose leisure to such an extent that the demand for goods, which may be high because of autonomous demand *g*, cannot be fully met. (Malinvaud, p. 85).

Malinvaud argues that the normal cyclical behaviour of the economy will be such that it moves between the Keynesian region and repressed inflation, as along the dotted line in figure 4.5. However, recent experience, partly explained by the terms of trade loss following the oil price rise, has included a significant dose of classical unemployment, i.e. excessive real wages. 'One may therefore understand why classical arguments about the causes of unemployment which fell into disrepute in the late forties are somewhat fashionable again.' (Malinvaud, p. 108)

The problem with this approach, of course, is that it still tells us nothing about the biggest problem of our time – inflation. The most important issue is not addressed at all, and that is: how can we best stimulate real output growth without raising inflation? If Keynes were alive today he would surely not have much truck with the assumption that prices are fixed and outputs are flexible in a period when output has been stagnant for a decade and we have experienced record inflation.

Summary

Keynesian economics is about deficiencies of aggregate demand. The popular model used to analyse this problem offered the simple solution that the government budget could compensate for these deficiencies. Recent reinterpretations of Keynes make the role of the budget less clear.

The greatest weaknesses in standard Keynesian thinking are with respect to the balance of payments and inflation. The latter is particularly problematic, as nominal money values are largely exogenous to the analytical system. The 1970s have seen a dramatic shift of the conventional wisdom away from the simple Keynesian story. This has been brought about as much by the weight of events as by the pressure of theoretical criticism.

5
Monetarists

The love of money and the love of learning seldom meet.
GEORGE HERBERT

'Monetarism' means many different things to different people
but more often than not, in the UK at least, it is a term of
abuse. On one extreme it could be thought of as covering the
complete utterances of Milton Friedman. On the other, it
could include only those who subscribe to the view that 'the
single necessary and sufficient condition for a sustained rise
in the money price level is a sustained increase in the normal
money stock.' Yet another definition, as seen in the previous
chapter, is belief in the stability of the demand for money
and controllability of the supply of money. It is of little value,
however, to pursue a precise definition of the term. What is
most important is to encompass the range of views about
how the economy works which typically fall within this
camp. As with other schools of thought, it may not be possible
to find particular individuals who subscribe to every aspect
of what follows, but at least it is fair to say that Monetarists
are united in giving the money stock an important role in their
implicit (or explicit) macroeconomic model, though the
emphasis in the Monetarist literature has changed considerably
in the last few years. Open economy aspects of Monetarism
will be pursued more fully in Chapter 7.

A further important point to notice is that the recent wave
of Monetarism in the UK spread from the USA. The prime

movers were mainly North Americans, or those who had studied in the USA. This of necessity made the early British Monetarists extra-establishment figures. They were not in a convenient political position to influence economic policy. The only real chance they had was to be right. The same could not be said of either the Keynesians or the New Cambridge group, who will be discussed below. They were very British phenomena who had easy access to the corridors of power. Only extreme incompetence could have denied them a ready audience in the UK.

Money in Static Models

It should be obvious that Model I has no room for a Monetarist interpretation since it has no explicit monetary sector or indeed assets of any kind. In Models II and III the cases which can be identified with Monetarism are often also called 'classical' cases.

The orthodox version of the classical case derives from what can be thought of as a special case of equation 1.9. This special case relates to what is commonly known as the quantity theory of money, though in classical economics it would be better called 'The Monetary Theory of the Price Level'. In modern economics it is part of the theory of the demand for real money balances. The quantity theory was based on an identity known as the equation of exchange.

5.1 $\qquad MV \equiv pT$

where M is the number of units of money in circulation, V is the number of times per period each unit is used (velocity), p is the average price level per unit transaction, and T is the number of unit transactions per period. This merely says that the value of money paid out in transactions is equal to the value of goods sold. The theory is achieved by adding the assumptions that V and T are constant, or at least exogenous to the monetary sector. Hence, we have a theory that prices are proportional to the money stock (which in a gold standard model was exogenous).

The modern version of the quantity theory is not based on the turnover of money like the equation of exchange, but rather on the average money balances demanded to be held. The primogenitor of demand for money function is, ironically, known as the Cambridge Equation, since it was associated with such famous Cambridge economists as Pigou and Robertson. The Cambridge Equation says either that individuals hold nominal money balances in proportion to their nominal income or that they hold real money balances in proportion to their real income.

5.2 $\quad M = kYp$

5.3 $\quad \dfrac{M}{p} = kY$

where M is the money stock, Y is income, p is the price level, and k is a constant. By the late 1950s, however, when Friedman tried to provide empirical support in the US for a relationship similar to 5.3, this equation was no longer part of the apparatus of Cambridge economists. Indeed, it was complete anathema to most of them.

The only differences between equation 5.3 and equation 1.11 are, first, that here income is not presumed to be fixed at its full employment level and, second, the interest rate is missing here. The implications of this for the IS–LM diagram are straightforward. If we consider the fixed price level case, it is clear in figure 1.2 that, if the demand for money does not depend upon the rate of interest, the demand-for-money line is vertical. This means that for each level of the money supply there is only one level of income at which the demand and supply of money will be equal. The implications for the LM curve are shown in figure 5.1. The LM curve is vertical.

The policy implications of this case of the model should be obvious. Monetary policy means changing the money supply which shifts the LM curve. Fiscal policy shifts the IS curve. If income is the target variable it is clear that fiscal policy will have no effect on income, only on the interest rate. Monetary policy is the tool needed to control income. It is worth noting that, while textbooks often call this the classical case, it is far from classical in the fixed price level

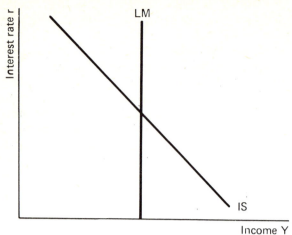

Figure 5.1

case. Only at full employment could figure 5.1 represent the classical case, and as a result monetary policy would only affect the price level and not real income.

It must be emphasised immediately that not even extreme Monetarists would be likely to subscribe to the vertical LM theory today. Although Friedman in his early empirical work in the US claimed to have estimated a demand-for-money function in which the interest rate was insignificant, the vast bulk of work done since has found the interest rate to be important. So, while this case is of historical interest, it need not be taken seriously as a practical possibility.

An alternative interpretation of the 'classical' case, and one which Monetarists may be more likely to subscribe to, can be thought of as being represented by Model IIIB. Here there is a supply side to the economy. Both labour supply and labour demand depend upon the *real* wage. This means that there is no change in aggregate output in response to shifts in aggregate demand. Changes in aggregate demand only affect the price level. This case is illustrated in figure 1.6 where S_B is the aggregate supply curve. A shift in aggregate demand from D_0 to D_1 will raise the price level from p_0 to p_1 but there will be no change in real income. This is actually a very significant piece of analysis and should be contrasted with the analysis in Model II, though it should be emphasised that even those who do subscribe to this view would regard it as a *long-run* case and not an accurate description of the short-run behaviour of the economy. We shall see in Chapter 8 how short-run behaviour is incorporated into this framework. In Model II there seemed to be an important distinction between monetary and fiscal policy. However, in Model III monetary and fiscal policy can be seen as merely complementary aspects of aggregate demand policy. Aggregate demand policy itself is of limited use, especially in Model IIIB, because real output is not affected in the long run by shifts in aggregate demand. Only the price level changes. Thus, even in this simple static model there would seem to be little milage to be obtained from making a critical distinction between monetary and fiscal policy. This point is reinforced when it is realised that the possibilities for independent monetary and fiscal policies are severly limited anyway. The government's budget deficit (i.e. the difference between tax revenue and government expenditure) is, after all, almost identical to the public sector borrowing requirement (PSBR). The PSBR has to be financed either by borrowing from the Bank of England (printing money) or by sales of government debt. Both of these have implications for the money supply, so it would be very difficult to control the money supply if there were a large PSBR.

To summarise so far, monetary policy is of no importance in Model I. In Model II there is a clear difference between monetary and fiscal policy and whichever is the more powerful in controlling national income depends on the shapes of the IS and LM curves. In Model IIIB real national output is independent of both monetary and fiscal policies in the aggregate. It is this last case which comes closest to the spirit of modern Monetarism, though there are many aspects of the latter which have still to be mentioned, especially with regard to the short-run behaviour of the economy.

The Real Balance Effect and The Transmission Mechanism

Important to an understanding of modern Monetarism is the story about how changes in the money supply are transmitted through the economy. The mechanism built into Models II and III is essentially the link proposed by Keynes which many would now see as insufficient. Basically, this relies upon changes in money stock first causing a portfolio disequilibrium. There is an excess money supply in portfolios and, therefore, excess demand for bonds. This leads to a rise in the price of bonds, which is equivalent to a fall in the rate of interest. The fall in the rate of interest then produces an increase in investment which through the multiplier effect influences income. As we have seen, much of the Keynesian disregard for monetary policy arose from the failure to find convincing evidence of a significant interest elasticity of investment expenditure. Many in the Monetarist camp, however, believe that the link from money to expenditure is much more direct. This direct link is often called the 'real balance effect'.

The earliest form of real balance effect was actually known as the Pigou Effect. This was usually applied to the behaviour of an economy in a depression when the price level was low. The effect arises because the low price level means that the real value of money balances is high. Consumers, in effect, make a capital gain on their money holdings and as a result spend more than they otherwise would for a given real income. The Pigou Effect was originally presented as an analytical device which would stabilise the macroeconomy, since it meant that prices would not fall indefinitely.

The real balance effect is more general than the Pigou Effect, though it relates to the same behavioural phenomenon. Anything which causes real money balances (or perhaps real liquid assets) to deviate from their desired level will cause a change in expenditures while the desired level of real balances is out of equilibrium. Thus a rise in the money supply could lead directly to an increase in expenditure. Instead of the excess money balances being reflected entirely as an excess demand for bonds, there would also be an excess demand for goods. The system as a whole cannot reduce its holdings of nominal money balances, so the excess real money balances have to be eliminated by either price level or real income increases until the nominal money supply is just demanded. Friedman has summarised this process as follows:

If individuals as a whole were to try to reduce the number of dollars they held, they could not all do so, they would simply be playing a game of musical chairs. In trying to do so, however, they would raise the flow of expenditures and of money incomes since each would be trying to spend more than he receives; in the process adding to someone else's receipts, and, reciprocally, finding his own higher than anticipated because of the attempt by still others to spend more than they receive. In the process, prices would tend to rise, which would reduce the real value of cash balances, that is, the quantity of goods and services that the cash balances will buy.

While individuals are thus frustrated in their attempt to reduce the number of dollars they hold, they succeed in achieving an equivalent change in their position, for the rise in money income and in prices reduces the ratio of these balances to their income and also the real value of these balances. The process will continue until this ratio and this real value are in accord with their desires. (M. Friedman, 1959, p. 609, Testimony in Hearings Before the Joint Economic Committee, Washington.)

There are considerable theoretical problems in specifying a real balance effect in a static macromodel, since it must of necessity be a disequilibrium phenomenon. The simplicity of the Keynesian model derives in large part from the separability of expenditures from the choice of financial assets. Indeed, Friedman's own permanent income theory of consumption implies that consumers' expenditure should be independent of asset composition. Nonetheless, several pieces of empirical work have purported to establish the existence of a real balance effect. Some models, such as Jonson (1976), have this running from real money balances to consumption, whilst others tend to have causation running from 'liquid assets' to consumption. Thus Townend (1976) includes lagged liquid assets in his consumption function and the 1977 version of HMT includes a distributed lag for 11 quarters on 'gross liquid assets of the personal sector.' However, this is clearly an area where further work is required of both a theoretical and empirical nature.

Modern Monetarism

The focus of attention of modern Monetarists has moved on from the framework of the IS—LM model. There are a number of reasons for this, among which are (a) the lack of dynamics, (b) the absence of a supply side to the model, (c) the absence of a government budget constraint, and (d) the inappropriateness of the model to an open economy. The lack of dynamics is particularly crucial since it is now the rate of inflation rather than the price level which is judged to be important, and expectations come to have a central role in behaviour. Contrast, for example, the following statement by Laidler with that from Friedman above:

> An increase in the rate of expansion of the money supply to a pace faster than that necessary to validate an ongoing anticipated inflation will first lead to a buildup of real money balances, whose implicit own rate of return will therefore begin to fall relative to that on other assets. As a consequence, a process of substitution into all other assets and into current consumption will be set in motion, with interest rates, both observable and unobservable, falling. The ensuing increase in current production will set in motion a multiplier process . . .
>
> Along with the increase in output just postulated goes a tendency for firms to increase their prices and for money wages to rise to levels in excess of the values these variables were initially expected to take. Given that there initially exists an expected rate of inflation, this involves an acceleration of the actual inflation rate relative to that expected rate. If the actual inflation rate influences the expected rate, the latter must also begin to rise. In its turn, an increase in the expected rate of inflation has two inter-related effects on variables involved in the transmission mechanism. It puts upward pressure on the rates of interest that assets denominated in nominal terms bear, and in increasing the opportunity cost of holding money, accentuates the very portfolio disequilibrium which sets going the first stage of the transmission mechanism and which accelerating inflation begins to offset. It also causes the inflation rate to accelerate further through its effect on price setting behaviour . . .
>
> Because . . . the expected and actual inflation rates will differ so long as output is not at its 'natural' level, the new equilibrium, like the initial one, will see the economy operating at such a level of real output. The expected rate of inflation will be higher in this new equilibrium, and so the quantity of real balances held by the public will be smaller. *If* money is 'super-neutral'[1] so that the 'natural' output level is independent of the inflation rate, and of any past history of disequilibrium in the economy (both of these being dubious assumptions supported by no empirical evidence of which I am aware, and the former being contradicted by a good deal of theoretical argument), then we would also expect to find real rates of interest returning to their initial levels, with nominal rates having increased

by the same amount as the inflation rate. If money is not 'super-neutral' then we might find real rates either higher or lower in the new equilibrium. In either event, though, a higher and more rapidly rising volume of nominal expenditure would be associated with higher nominal interest rates. If real balances are to be lower in the new equilibrium, then, on average, during the transition towards it, the rate of inflation must exceed the rate of monetary expansion. Moreover, if nominal interest rates at first fall, but end up at a level higher than that ruling initially, they must on average rise during the transition. (Laidler 1978a, pp. 170−1.)

It is clear that Monetarism has developed a great deal in the past 20 years. Indeed, it is hard to find a description of price and output dynamics of comparable detail from any other school of thought in the UK. Two important issues arising will be discussed further below in the chapters on inflation and the balance of payments (Chapters 7 and 8). These are the questions of the 'natural' rate of unemployment and of the influence of the exchange rate on the transmission mechanism. One issue which must be discussed here, however, is the question of 'rational expectations' formation.

As can be seen from the Laidler quote, expectations have come to have increasing importance in the story of price and output dynamics. One hypothesis which has become associated with extreme versions of monetarism is known as the 'rational expectations' approach. This assumes that all agents in the economy are endowed with all available information including the model of how the economy works. They will, thus, not make *systematic* errors in forming expectations but will on average be correct, subject to a *random* error. If there is any truth in this approach, which is a point of controversy even among Monetarists, its implications for understanding the power of, say, monetary policy are very considerable. Suppose, for example, that the transmission mechanism outlined above is basically correct and actors know it to be so. They will forecast money supply changes using all available information, such as the budget deficit, balance of payments, and any announcement of intentions which the authorities have made.

However, forecast changes in the money supply impinge directly upon money income through the effect of expectations on prices. Only changes in the rate of monetary expansion that are not forecast have their effects transmitted to money income through the traditional channels of portfolio disequilibrium, output changes, and price reactions to output disequilibrium. Thus, the extent to which a particular change in the monetary expansion rate is divided up between a forecast component and an unforeseen one will influence the way its effects are transmitted. This division of course depends upon the way in which agents themselves form their expectations, and we have empirical evidence consistent with the view that this in turn depends upon such things as the way in which the authorities finance their deficits and conduct themselves in the foreign exchange market. In short, the nature of the transmission mechanism for monetary policy itself depends upon the manner in which monetary policy is carried out and the way in which it interacts with fiscal and exchange rate policy. (Laidler, *op cit*, p. 184.)

The implication of this statement is quite simple and rather perplexing, though it should be considered as a serious possibility. Since private actors in the system try to form expectations on the basis of all available information and the best available model, they must 'rationally' attempt to anticipate the behaviour of the government itself. The potency of policy (particularly monetary) depends on the extent to which it is unanticipated. At the very least this would seem to suggest that we should model the public sector as an endogenous entity which interacts with the private sector. Policy instruments can no longer be regarded as entirely exogenous influences. At worst, however, the rational expectations philosophy represents a devastating critique of the rationale for Keynesian-type budgetary policy which makes no allowance for the fact that the private sector will anticipate the behaviour of the government itself.

The implications of the rational expectations approach are far from worked out. The recent interest has been stimulated by papers such as Sargent and Wallace (1975). Its empirical validity in wide areas of economics has yet to be seriously tested. Nonetheless, the idea clearly has an importance for the theoretical development of macroeconomics, not because it is correct, but rather because it provides a polar case to the one which has dominated thinking in the area since the Second World War. We can only use our judgment effectively to analyse real-world situations if we understand the full logical implications of all the alternative paradigms available.

Demand for Money

It would be a misrepresentation of the Monetarist story to move on without saying something about the demand for money. One major tenet of the Monetarist tradition is that the demand for money is a stable function of a few variables. This contention was supported by a considerable amount of empirical work in the US in the late 1950s and the 1960s. A typical functional form for the relationship was

5.4 $$\frac{M}{p} = \alpha Y^{\beta} r^{\gamma}$$

which, when all variables were transformed into logarithms, could be estimated as

5.5 $$\ln \frac{M}{p} = \alpha + \beta \ln Y + \gamma \ln r$$

where M is the nominal money stock, p is a price index, Y is GDP and r is an interest rate on a substitute asset. One simple modification of this formulation involves the assumption that equation 5.4 is a desired demand level but that the actual holding is only partially adjusted towards this. As a result, equation 5.5 would have to include a lagged dependent variable on the right-hand side.

Little attention has traditionally been paid to the fact that both Y and r are endogenous variables. This means that estimation of equation 5.5 by ordinary least squares yields biased and inconsistent estimates of α, β and γ, owing to the existence of simultaneous equation bias. However, even more serious, as at least one interpretation of events indicates, is the question of identification. Whether or not equation 5.5 can be estimated correctly as it is depends upon what supply conditions are presumed to be. In principle, equation 5.5 alone could be a demand function, a supply function or some combination of the two. The assumption usually used to identify equation 5.5 as a demand function was that money supply was demand determined. Under fixed exchange rates, interest rates were primarily determined exogenously or with regard to the capital account of the balance of payments. To maintain interest rates at their target level, the authorities had to supply the money that was demanded.

It should be no surprise to learn that relationships such as equation 5.5 broke down in the early 1970s. This follows both a change in exchange rate policy and the change in domestic monetary policy known as competition and credit control. (Indeed, several major macroeconomic relationships have broken down in the early 1970s, including the consumption function and the simple Phillips curve.) The breakdown was particularly bad when using M3, the broader definition of money, which includes interest-bearing time deposits as well as current account deposits. However, this is not surprising in the period when banks started to use interest rates to attract deposits. The mere fact that money demand equations which fitted well on earlier data broke down in the early 1970s should not be taken as evidence that such functions no longer exist. The truth may be simply that structural changes made the old estimation techniques inappropriate.

It has been shown by Artis and Lewis (1976) that a stable relationship can be fitted. They drop the assumption that the money stock is demand determined and substitute for it the assumption that supply is exogenous. The equation to be estimated is then an interest rate adjustment equation rather than a money demand equation. Its form is

$$5.6 \quad \ln r = \alpha + \beta \ln Y + \gamma \ln M + \delta \ln r_{t-1}$$

They show that this fits well for periods which include data from after 1971 as well as from before. Finally, however, it is worth noting that Hendry and Mizon (1978) present estimates of a demand for money function fitted to both pre- and post-1971 data. This has a more complex dynamic form than equation 5.5 and it appears to fit the data well, without making any allowances for structural change.

The Real Effects of Money

Finally, it is worth attempting a caricature of the major

different views commonly found about the effects of changes in monetary variables upon the real economy. Let us consider the experiment to consist of a once-and-for-all rise in the money stock which is announced in advance. What will be the effect on real output and real incomes? Most economists would no doubt distinguish between short-run effects and long-run effects, though it would be doubtful if agreement could be reached about what is meant by 'long-run'. Monetarists often define the long run as being the period over which money is neutral, i.e. the period over which expectations are formed correctly. However, that will not do because we are then left with a tautology. Let us then take short-run as one year and long-run as five years and take the liberty of reading between the lines of the written work of subscribers to various views. Four groups will be distinguished: orthodox Monetarists, extreme (rational expectations) Monetarists, orthodox (especially US) Keynesians and extreme Keynesians. Their likely views are set out in Table 5.1.

Table 5.1 Effect of change in money stock on real income and output

Group	Short-run 1 year	Long-run 5 years
Extreme 'rational expectations' Monetarist e.g. Sargent and Wallace (1975)	None unless unanticipated	None
Orthodox Monetarist e.g. Laidler (1978b)	Significant effects	Small effect diminishing over time to nothing. Definitely smaller than short-run.
Orthodox, or US Keynesian e.g. Modigliani (1977) Blinder (1978)	Small effect	Small effect, but probably greater than short-run.
Extreme Keynesian e.g. Kaldor (1970)	No effect, causation wrong way round.	No effect, causation wrong way round.

The only apparent agreement is between extreme Monetarists and extreme Keynesians. These conclusions are of course based on very different reasoning. The former rely upon the increase in money stock being anticipated and therefore reflected in price setting behaviour but not in real output or income. The latter rely on the proposition that 'money' is not an artifact that can be meaningfully defined or controlled and is merely a meaningless by-product of financial intermediation. Orthodox Monetarists believe that whatever real effects there are occur fairly quickly and that these die out as time goes on so that eventually there is no real change. This is because of the impact of the real balance effect followed by a slow catch up of expectations. Orthodox Keynesians believe that the real effects take time to build up because investment expenditures respond slowly to lower interest rates. Some in this group may, however, agree that eventually the effect will become zero.

Only extreme Keynesians would presumably dispute the effect of such a change in the money stock on the price level. Most orthodox Keynesians and Monetarists would agree that this effect starts slowly and gradually builds up, reaching a maximum in the long run, but getting most of the way there in a moderate period of three or four years. Extreme Monetarists would, of course, see the price level adjustment as being almost immediate.

Summary

An understanding of modern Monetarism must be based on a clear distinction between short and long run, between open and closed economies and, for open economies, between fixed and floating exchange rate cases. The open economy issue has not been discussed in this chapter — it will be pursued in Chapter 7.

The long-run case closest to the spirit of Monetarism is where money is neutral and aggregate supply is determined independent of aggregate demand. The latter merely determines the price level. The short-run story depends upon what is presumed about the process of price expectation formation.

Note

1. 'Super' neutrality means dynamic neutrality, i.e. the effect of a change in the *rate* of *growth* of money on real output.

6

New Cambridge[1]

Lear: *Now our joy . . . what can you say to draw a third more
   opulent than your sisters?*
Cordelia: *Nothing, my Lord . . .*
Lear: *Nothing will come of nothing: speak again.*

The term 'New Cambridge' applies to the combined utterances
of the Cambridge Economic Policy Group (CEPG) under the
leadership of Wynne Godley. They are the Young Pretenders
of the Keynesian tradition. For a long time they had not
published their ideas in terms of a formal model so it was
difficult to assess their contribution, but this position changed
with the publication of Cripps and Godley (1976). They
became particularly famous for pointing out a relationship
between the balance of payments deficit and the budget
deficit, a relationship which events have made them de-
emphasise. They also gained notoriety by proposing import
controls as a cure for the UK balance of payments problems
of 1974–6, a solution which, incidentally, is inconsistent with
their earlier attribution of the balance of payments deficit to
the budget deficit, though their interest in import controls
has not declined in line with the decline in the balance of
payments deficit.

The balance of payments aspect of New Cambridge will be
discussed in Chapter 7. In this chapter we will first present a
brief sketch of the evolution of the New Cambridge approach
to macroeconomics, and then concentrate on outlining what
seem to be the three novel characteristics of their model:
the aggregate expenditure function, the determination of

money wages and the influence of income distribution, though most attention will be directed at the first of these, which is admitted to be the distinguishing feature of the group.

Evolution of New Cambridge

It is generally acknowledged that the origins of New Cambridge owe a great deal to Kaldor, and in particular to his argument concerning export-led growth. He was repeatedly critical of demand management policy which tried to expand the economy through fiscal stimulus to domestic consumption. The effect of this was always to raise imports faster than exports so that the expansion of the economy was always cut short because of the recurrence of balance of payments problems. The growth of the economy was in practice constrained by the rate of growth of exports. Only if domestic demand were expanded as a result of a growth in exports, rather than domestic consumption, could the economy enter a period of sustained growth. Kaldor (1971) pointed out the result of this policy failure which was that: 'The ratio of consumption to GDP in Britain is still appreciably higher, and that of investment lower, than in all the industrialized countries with higher trend rates of growth.'

It is also possible to attribute to Kaldor the New Cambridge orientation towards the sectoral balance sheet identity. In a letter to *The Times* on 30 March 1973 he wrote:

> By the laws of arithmetic (which are more dependable than the laws of economics) a £3,000m financial deficit in the public sector must have its exact counterpart in the 'net acquisition of financial assets' by the personal sector, the company sector and the overseas sector. The latter is the obverse of the balance of payments on current account. Since with the squeeze on real incomes through incomes policy one cannot hope for any large increase in personal saving ... this policy must involve either a vast increase in profits in excess of industry's financial requirements or a vast deterioration in the balance of payments or some combination of the two.

This line of approach, which is obviously based on an identity, when combined with Neild's observation that 'the personal sector's financial balance has been remarkably stable since

1961,' (*The Times*, 19/20 July 1973) plus a certain amount of licence, transforms into the famous statement by Godley and Cripps that

> [It is] a false assumption which has dominated policy making for many years that the balance of payments is determined as much by events abroad, domestic costs and the exchange rate as by fiscal and monetary decisions at home ... The contention that other than in the short term, the private sector shows a small and stable surplus, implies that *the public sector's budget deficit fully determines the current balance of payments:* given the size of the budget deficit, changes in exports, import prices, etc. make a lot of difference to real income and output, but none at all to the balance of payments, however paradoxical this may at first appear ... (*The Times*, 22/23 January 1974.)

Notice that where Neild referred to the *personal* sector balance being stable, we now have the *private* sector showing a small and stable surplus. The policy conclusion, as emphasised by Neild, was that 'The budget should be used to determine the foreign balance and the exchange rate to determine the level of activity' (Letter to *The Times*, 26 February 1974). This of course is entirely contrary to Keynes' own view of the budget as 'pump priming'.

The first econometric evidence in support of their view was presented by Godley, Cripps and Fetherston in their evidence to the Expenditure Committee of the House of Commons (HC328, July 1974). There they summarise their central contention to be that 'private sector's net acquisition of financial assets ... is likely to be *fairly small and predictable*'. As a result they could not only check the consistency of the government's own budget and balance of payments forecasts but they could also 'infer with a fair degree of accuracy, what the official forecast of the balance of payments ... is or ought to be'. The apparent evidence of a stable private sector surplus led them to the inevitable conclusion that 'the only potentially destabilising agents are the government's own actions with regard to expenditure taxation and credit on the one hand, and, on the other, foreign influences, particularly export demand and world commodity prices'. Their policy recommendation was that, 'given that decisions about public expenditure have been taken, and given that the government is prepared to specify its targets with respect to the balance of trade and employment, an appropriate ('par') rate of tax may be inferred which should not normally be changed for stabilization reasons'. In other words, the government should not attempt to 'stabilise' the economy by using discretionary policy changes. Rather, for a given level of government expenditure, they should set tax rates so that they yield an appropriate budget deficit at *full employment* — what is appropriate being determined by the average private sector surplus. Any rise in the budget deficit will then reflect deviations of national income from full employment and will provide an automatic stabiliser. A fuller analysis of this idea of a 'full-employment' budget deficit is provided in Neild and Ward (1978).

New Cambridge economists had a good year in 1974 when the budget deficit of £5 billion was associated with a balance of payments deficit of nearly £4 billion. However, there can be little doubt that since that time events have been less kind to them. In the financial year 1975/6 the budget deficit rose to about £10 billion whereas the balance of payments deficit shrank to about £1 billion. Bispham can be forgiven for concluding that the empirical basis of New Cambridge had 'broken down massively' (NIER, November 1975). The 'laws of arithmetic' had not broken down, rather the private sector net acquisition of financial assets had risen from less than 3% of GDP in 1974 to in excess of 6% of GDP in 1975. It was obviously not quite as small or stable (or even predictable) as had been thought.

Since that episode the CEPG has retreated somewhat from its earlier position and has rightly concentrated on the exposition of more detailed forecasts in conjunction with the evolution of an explicit forecasting model. 'In its broad structure the CEPG model lies squarely within the postwar tradition of Keynesian model-building' (Cripps and Godley 1976, p. 9). By this is meant that it is basically an income—expenditure flow model with no explicit financial sector or supply side. A complete outline of this model will not be attempted here; rather it is adequate to concentrate on its novel features.

The Aggregate Expenditure Function

The argument that the private sector has a fairly small and predictable surplus has now been turned around to make the essential distinguishing feature of New Cambridge. It was seen in Chapters 1 and 2 that, whereas typical textbook models have one relationship for consumption and one for investment, forecasters have usually considered it appropriate to further disaggregate each category of expenditure. HMT, for example, now has two categories of consumption in addition to several categories of investment and stockbuilding. The CEPG bases its approach on a single aggregate expenditure relationship for the whole private sector. Thus their dependent variable is the sum of all personal consumption expenditure, investment by firms and stockbuilding. More explicitly, the assumption of a small surplus implies 'the explicit hypothesis associated with the term "New Cambridge" [is] that virtually all disposable income of the private sector as a whole will be spent on goods and services with a fairly short lag' (Fetherston and Godley 1978).

The first published estimate of the aggregate expenditure function was submitted as evidence to the Public Expenditure Committee in 1974. It is:

6.1 $$PX_t = 0.533(Y-T)_t + 0.416(Y-T)_{t-1}$$
$$(10.08) \qquad (7.81)$$

$$+ 0.899HP_t + 0.79BA_t + 0.962S_t$$
$$(3.13) \qquad (3.68) \qquad (13.08)$$

Total real private sector expenditure, PX, depends upon current and last year's real private disposable income, $Y - T$, plus the net increase in personal hire purchase debt, HP, plus the net increase in bank advances and loans to the personal sector, BA, plus the increase in the value of stocks and work in progress, S.

There are two points worth noticing. The first is that if the aggregation has really taken in the entire private sector then it should include financial institutions as being within the sector. That being so, HP and BA should not appear in the equation, as the sum of these for the private sector as a whole is zero (apart from net foreign lending). There may be some justification for the inclusion of these terms, but CEPG do not say what it is. At the very least it is hard to believe that they are really exogenous variables. A fuller discussion of this point is available in Rowan (1976).

The second point is rather simple, but it requires rather complicated argument to explain its full implications. The student with no background in econometrics may, therefore, find that the following discussion becomes a bit difficult. The point is that the core of equation 6.1 is very close in form to the national income accounting identity. Since the identity is known to hold exactly, with certainty, it is far from clear that equation 6.1 is an estimate of a behavioural relationship rather than the result of approximating an identity. As a result there should be some doubt as to whether these numbers have any behavioural significance whatever. The CEPG interpret the fact that the sum of the coefficients on current and lagged income add to near unity to mean that any change in current income is very quickly converted into expenditure. However, a good reason to doubt this interpretation is that it is in stark contrast to all other work on consumption and investment over the last two decades or so which has discovered how sticky these expenditures are.

Consider a truncated version of equation 6.1

$$6.2 \qquad PX_t = \alpha(Y - T)_t + S_t$$

Consider also the national income accounting identity (time subscripts are dropped)

$$6.3 \qquad Y \equiv C + I + G + X - P$$

or, equivalently,

$$6.4 \qquad C + I \equiv Y - G - X + P$$

add stockbuilding to both sides

$$6.5 \qquad C + I + S = Y - G + S - X + P$$

we also have the definition of PX, which is

6.6 $\quad PX \equiv C + I + S$

so equation 6.5 can be expressed as

6.7 $\quad PX \equiv (Y - G) + S + (P - X)$

It is hard to escape the observation that equations 6.7 and 6.2 are very similar. However, equation 6.7 is known to hold exactly for any time period we care to choose. The only difference is that equation 6.7 has an extra term in the balance of payments and has G instead of T. Nonetheless, if the balance of payments were a random variable with mean zero and the budget were *approximately* balanced, there would be a strong presumption that the estimate of α in equation 6.2 would be close to unity. Any deviation from unity would, in fact, say more about the budget and the balance of payments than it would about the behaviour of the private sector. This point need not detain us, however, because using the original CEPG annual data for 1954–72, an ordinary least squares estimate of equation 6.1 gives the following results:

6.8 $\quad PX_t = 0.92(Y-T)_t + 0.04(Y-T)_{t-1} - 0.22HP_t$
$\qquad\quad$ (12) $\qquad\qquad$ (0.5) $\qquad\qquad\qquad$ (−0.14)

$\qquad\quad - 0.98BA_t + 0.39S_t$
$\qquad\qquad$ (−1.1) $\qquad$ (1.9)

$\qquad\quad R^2 = 0.9999 \qquad t$ stats in parentheses

In effect, only the variables in equation 6.2 have any significant role in this equation and the estimated value of α is clearly not significantly different from unity. This combined with the high R^2 suggests very strongly that we are picking up the relationship imposed by the identity. A comparable result can be achieved if a similar equation is fitted to US data for 1954–74, again using ordinary least squares:

6.9 $\quad PX_t = 20.6 + 1.3(Y-T)_t + 0.08(Y-T)_{t-1}$
$\qquad\quad$ (0.99) (2.4) $\qquad\qquad$ (0.18)

$$-0.53(Y-T)_{t-2} + 0.76HP_t - 0.42S_t$$
$$(1.3) \qquad (0.72) \qquad (0.43)$$

$$R^2 = 0.999$$

Again the overall fit as judged by R^2 is very good, but $(Y-T)_t$ is the dominant explanatory variable and the coefficient on it is not significantly different from unity.

How then do the CEPG produce the estimation results in equation 6.1 which seem to be at such variance with the results quoted here? It could be simply that the estimation technique used here is inappropriate because it does not correct for simultaneous equation bias. However, the dominant characteristic of the problem seems to be the close correlation between PX_t and $(Y-T)_t$ rather than correlation between $(Y-T)_t$ and the equation error. A more likely explanation would appear to be that CEPG themselves adjust for simultaneous equation bias in a most extraordinary way. What they do is to impose an additional condition in the estimation of equation 6.1 which is that:

6.10 $\quad (Y-T)_t = 0.42PX_t + X_t$

where X_t represents other exogenous determinants of income and the coefficient 0.42 'is chosen *a priori*.' To make matters worse CEPG do not add a genuine series of data on exogenous expenditures to incorporate in the estimation of equation 6.1 and 6.10, rather they seem to define the X_t variable by equation 6.10. As a result they are merely restricting the results in 6.1 and *not correcting for simultaneous equation bias at all*. For example, in an unpublished paper explaining their technique, Fetherston (1975) states: 'The exogenous variables (including stochastic terms) subsumed in X_t do not need to be specified *at all* — so that no observations on them are necessary to obtain parameter estimates.' The effect of adding this as a restriction rather than estimating by two-stage least squares, or some other *genuine* simultaneous equation technique, is merely to restrict the size of the coefficient on $(Y-T)_t$ in equation 6.1, and thus to increase the contribution of the remaining variables in the equation. $(Y-T)_{t-1}$ being highly correlated with $(Y-T)_t$ now takes on a coefficient to compensate for what the coefficient on $(Y-T)_t$ would be if it were unrestricted. The fact that these two coefficients sum to unity has exactly the same significance as the unit coefficients in equations 6.8 and 6.9 — in behavioural terms, none at all.

Even the CEPG were not immune to the fact that their equation did not fit well for subsequent years and in 1976 they published a new version which was

6.8 $$PX_t = 0.6163(Y-T)_t + 0.3605(Y-T)_{t-1}$$
$$\quad\;\; (7.6) \qquad\qquad (4.09)$$

$$+ \; 1.173HP_t + 0.4772S_t - 156.5$$
$$(2.26) \qquad (4.99) \qquad (1.14)$$

However, in order to improve the fit they found it necessary to measure variables in nominal rather than real terms, a procedure which is usually avoided on the grounds that it produces spurious correlations between otherwise unrelated variables.

As a theoretical justification of their expenditure function CEPG have offered a kind of latter day Cambridge equation (*Economic Policy Review* 1976, p. 49). This says that for the private sector the net stock of financial assets, FA, plus a proportion β of stocks, H, will be equal to a proportion α of private disposable income, $(Y-T)$.

6.12 $$FA + \beta H = \alpha(Y-T)$$

Since $\Delta FA = NAFA$ (net acquisition of financial assets), and $\Delta H = S$ (stockbuilding), taking first differences of 6.12 gives:

$$NAFA + \beta S = \alpha \left[(Y-T)_t - (Y-T)_{t-1} \right]$$

and given that $NAFA_t \equiv (Y-T)_t - PX_t$ it follows that

6.13 $$PX_t = (1-\alpha)(Y-T)_t + \alpha(Y-T)_{t-1} + \beta S_t$$

The basic underlying hypothesis then is that for the private sector as a whole there is a stable demand function for its net stock of financial assets and that this demand is strictly proportional to private disposable income. As an empirical proposition it is added that any adjustment of that stock to a disequilibrium occurs rapidly. Even Monetarists would surely flinch at such oversimplification.

Inflation, Wages and Income Distribution

It is not necessary to spend a great deal of time discussing the CEPG approach to inflation, since they do not seem to regard it as a major distinguishing feature of their group. However, it is convenient to sketch it at this stage and return to the inflation question later. In line with the drift of UK Keynesianism, the dominant drive for inflation is arbitrary and exogenous. However, the system is far from neutral with respect to price level changes. Price level increases raise the demand for nominal financial assets and thereby reduce the level of current *real* expenditures, i.e. there is a real balance effect. Cripps and Godley summarise their approach in the following terms.

... Money wage determination is represented as the outcome of periodic negotiated wage settlements composed in part of compensation for past price and tax changes and in part of *ex ante* changes in the disposable real wage. ... Under the CEPG assumptions a lower rate of unemployment (given the balance of payments and terms of trade) would normally be associated with a slower rate of inflation ... Given the view that money wage bargaining is concerned with real wage targets, income distribution is of particular importance because it directly affects resources available for real wages, and hence the inflation rate. (Cripps and Godley 1976.)

There are really four elements to the CEPG inflation process. These are:

1. The average time elapsed since settlements were negotiated (γ_0)
2. The tax rate on wages (t_w)
3. The actual real wage rate after tax (WD)
4. The target real disposable wage (WD^*)

The actual total real wage bill is determined as a residual

from national income after deducting taxes and profits. Workers are assumed to look at their real take-home pay and to compare this with their target real wage. The bigger the discrepancy between the actual and the target, the faster will be the rate of inflation — the actual adjustment speed presumably depending upon γ_0. The actual inflation rate is given by:

$$6.14 \qquad r = \frac{1}{\gamma_0} \left(1 - \frac{WD}{WD*}\right)$$

Clearly, the critical driving force in this process is the target real wage (though for a given national income anything which takes resources away from workers will immediately raise the inflation rate). However, 'the factors determining the target real wage cannot be formulated with any precision. In particular, it has not been perceptibly influenced by the level of unemployment' (Cripps and Godley 1976, p. 342).

Further comment is difficult since the critical factor which explains all is by way of a *deus ex machina;* however, it is clear that the reason they get a *positive* relationship between unemployment and inflation is that higher unemployment reduces the real wage bill and so *increases* bargaining pressure for the fixed real wage target. The strangest thing of all perhaps is that unions bargain for a real wage *bill* and not a real wage *rate*.

A US Keynesian view of New Cambridge

It may be helpful to report the assessment of a prominent US Keynesian economist, Alan Blinder, of the version of the CEPG model presented by Fetherston and Godley to a conference in the United States:

> In reviewing the differences between the Fetherston—Godley model and Keynesian economics as it is now practised in the US, I am struck by how many aspects have already been jettisoned here, often after a great controversy: the completely passive supply side, the fixed interest rate, the interest-inelastic investment demand, the trivialization of monetary policy, and so on. Revising any of these hypotheses would seem to be taking a step backward.

In comparing the dynamic properties of the CEPG model with American Keynesian models, Blinder has three main points:

First, ... the adjustment of asset holdings to income flows is remarkably fast. In US models like the MPS model, it may take years for the desired assets income ratio to be restored after a shock upsets it; in the Fetherston—Godley model, this process takes a single year. Second, there is no treatment of inflationary expectations when the model is out of steady state equilibrium (where inflation must be zero). ... Third, the responses of wages and prices to shocks come much faster in the Fetherston—Godley model than they do in American Keynesian models. The contrast is especially marked in wages, where the glacial response of money wages in the US stands in sharp relief to the one-year lag in the Fetherston— Godley model. In addition, because the Marshallian scissors have been broken in two, shocks on the demand side of the economy ... do not spill over to the supply side and thus cannot kick off a spell of inflation.
The differences can be appreciated by considering the dynamic multipliers for a change in public expenditures. In the Fetherston— Godley model, real output rises substantially at the outset and even more in the long run. The price level never moves. In modern American Keynesian models, real output effects would build for a while, and then decline toward zero (the 'natural rate' hypothesis). The price level, on the other hand, would show little response at first, but a substantial response over the long run. Were I giving advice to government officials, I would stick to the implications of the American Keynesian models. (Blinder 1978, p. 82.)

Blinder's comments on the New Cambridge analysis of import controls are quoted in Chapter 7.

Summary

One of the major distinguishing characteristics of the New Cambridge group has been their approach to the balance of payments. This will be discussed in Chapter 7. The characteristic of their formal model which is most unusual is their aggregate expenditure function. It has been argued that there is good reason to question both the validity of their estimates of this and the interpretation which they place upon them. While there is good reason to doubt the value of their contribution to building formal macroeconomic models, this does not mean that they have not had important things to say about current issues. It is merely that the things they get right do not follow because they have in any sense got a 'better' model. They were, for example, in agreement with Monetarists in pointing to the importance of a longer term view of macroeconomic policy. Godley, in particular, was one of the first to point out the dangers of public expenditure growth due to inflation supplementation (this led to the introduction of cash limits). The CEPG has also done important work on clarifying the correct measure of fiscal policy stance associated with the 'full employment budget deficit.'

Nonetheless, schools of thought survive because of the value of an analytical framework and there can be little doubt that the formal innovations proposed by New Cambridge are of dubious value. The value of the group to date has been in its informed comments on current events; these will not outlive them.

Note

1. This chapter owes a great deal to unpublished material prepared for undergraduate research projects at the University of Essex by Chris Boyd, Chris Ellis and Marilyn Sullivan. Boyd collected some of the quotations and estimated the expenditure function for the US. Sullivan estimated the expenditure function for the UK. The latter was replicated independently by Ellis and corrected for first-order autocorrelation, though this result is not reported.

PART III
Issues

In Part II the main approaches of various groups were set out, at least in so far as their overall view of the economy is concerned. Many aspects of the different views are, however, yet to be pursued and it is convenient to do this by reference to the major macroeconomic policy issues of our time. Part III, therefore, discusses the issues of balance of payments, inflation, crowding out and fine tuning. The first two are problems in themselves; the second two relate to the proper role of the government. Then there is an example in Chapter 11 of how we might analyse the effects of a major shock such as the oil crisis or the North Sea oil discovery. Finally, Chapter 12 presents a view of the development of UK macroeconomics which seems to be justified by the contents of this book.

7
Balance of Payments

Then at the balance let's be mute,
We never can adjust it;
What's done we partly may compute,
But know not what's resisted.
ROBERT BURNS

Few could question that the balance of payments had been a dominating and recurrent problem in the UK up to the late 1970s for as long as anyone could remember. Later in this chapter we shall consider why it is that the balance of payments is a problem, but first it is convenient to outline how the balance of payments has been viewed in the context of macroeconomic models. A number of approaches which have appeared mainly in the 'trade theory' literature rather then in macroeconomics, such as the elasticities and absorption approaches, will be dealt with only tangentially *en passant* where they are relevant.

The Keynesian or Structural Approach

The Keynesian approach is based upon an analysis of the balance of trade. In its simplest form it relies on a single import function and a single export function such as equations 1.3 and 1.4. If we specify the import function so that imports are proportional to income as in equation 1.3,

7.1 $\qquad P = \gamma Y$

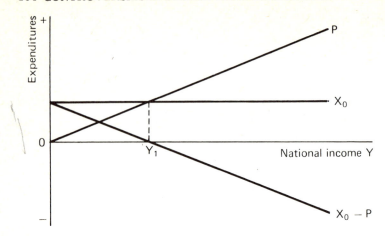

Figure 7.1

while exports, X_0, remain exogenously determined, then the balance of payments can be analysed simply in the context of figure 7.1. Since exports are constant and imports rise with national income, the balance of payments gets steadily worse as national income rises. Beyond a national income of Y_1 the balance of payments is in deficit.

While this model is a gross over-simplification, it is based on a view of the economy which is widely held and which would appear to be substantially justified by UK experience. This is that any tendency for over-expansion in the UK economy produces balance of payments problems. The experience of the Stop–Go cycle in the UK throughout the 1950s and 1960s seemed to confirm the story that domestic expansion increases imports faster than exports, so the balance of payments inevitably deteriorates. As a result, the expansion has to be reversed. One curiosity, however, to which we shall return, is why it is that this pattern does not seem to apply to other countries? How can it be that countries like West Germany and Japan can expand so fast without running into balance of payments problems? Indeed, West Germany clearly has exactly the opposite problem – its economic success is associated with an almost perpetual balance of payments surplus.

Although the forecasting model of Chapter 2 is far more

complex in detail it has basically the same properties. Rather than a single import and export function each of these is broken down into several categories. Each export category typically depends on foreign demand and relative prices and each import category depends upon domestic demand and relative prices. The overall balance of payments forecast is obtained by combining all of these expenditure categories which have been forecast separately. Hence it is sometimes called the 'structural' approach to the balance of payments, since the aggregate is built up from many smaller elements.

The properties of the forecasting model are very similar to the simple expenditure model. An expansion of domestic aggregate demand worsens the balance of payments and the addition of a relative price effect can only serve to reinforce this (even if inflation is largely exogenous!). However, the structural approach to the balance of payments does allow a bias to develop in attributing blame for balance of payments problems. Since the core of the balance of payments is the real trade account, failure here must be due to 'inadequate' export performance, these inadequacies being attributable either to unenterprising businessmen or myopic trade unions who bid up wages and make export prices 'uncompetitive'. At least two other approaches (New Cambridge and Monetarist) point the finger directly at government macroeconomic policy as the source of the problem.

Mundell's Assignment Problem

One major inadequacy of the Keynesian approach to the balance of payments is that it focuses entirely upon the current account. Systematic interactions between the capital account and the domestic economy are thereby completely ignored. A simple rectification of this omission, in the IS–LM framework, was proposed by Mundell (1968). This treatment still provides the basis of many textbook models of the balance of payments. Ignoring capital flows was, perhaps, excusable in the 1950s since there was not general convertibility of major currencies and, as a result, private capital flows were of minimal significance. However, by

1971 financial capital movements were potentially so large
that many observers attributed the breakdown of the fixed
exchange rate system to their very size and volatility.

The Mundell model is achieved by adding to Model II of
Chapter 1 a relationship between net capital flows and the
domestic interest rate:

7.2 $\quad k = f(r)$

Net capital flows depend upon the interest rate.

Capital flows should not be thought of as sales of machines
to foreigners, rather they are net sales to foreigners of domestic bonds. There is obviously a problem in drawing the line
between the current and capital accounts, and in this case
'capital' includes only financial assets. Assuming foreign
interest rates to be fixed exogenously, as the domestic
interest rate rises foreigners will buy more domestic bonds
so the capital account of the balance of payments will improve. In effect, foreigners are lending more to the domestic
economy.

The overall balance of payments is the current account
plus the capital account. The current account gets worse as
national income rises just as in the Keynesian model. Thus,
if balance of payments equilibrium is to be maintained
(at zero overall) as national income rises, the domestic
rate of interest must also rise so that the improved capital
account compensates for the worsening current account.
In other words, the locus of zero overall balance of payments
positions will be a positive relationship between national
income and the interest rate, like BB in figure 7.2.

Equilibrium for the system as a whole requires that all
three lines BB, LM and IS should intersect at the same point.
Consider the policy choices in the initial situation depicted
in figure 7.2. The IS and LM curves intersect at A where
there is full employment. However, this is not a point of balance of payments equilibrium, since A is to the right of the
BB curve. In fact there is a balance of payments deficit at A
equal to the horizontal distance between A and BB multi-
plied by the marginal propensity to import. It is open to the
authorities to correct the deficit by appropriate use of

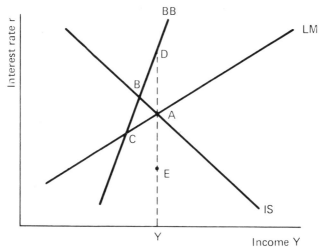

Figure 7.2

monetary and fiscal policy, but it is not obvious which to use.

A fiscal deflation would move the economy to point C, whereas a contraction of the money supply would move it to point B. Mundell's point is that the best response is to react with monetary policy to the balance of payments and with fiscal policy to output (and thus to unemployment). Consider the contrary. Initially we react to the balance of payments deficit by shifting IS down until it passes through C. This has corrected the balance of payments but caused unemployment. An increase in money supply now designed to eliminate unemployment would shift the LM curve down to the right. The economy would then be at a point like E where the balance of payments deficit is *worse* than it was originally. If, however, starting from A we change the money supply in response to a balance of payments deficit and fiscal policy in response to unemployment , the economy would converge on point D at which there is full employment and balance of payments equilibrium. This is the reason for Mundell's assignment of monetary policy to the balance of payments and fiscal policy to output and employment. This can be contrasted with the New Cambridge view that 'the budget should be used to determine the foreign balance,' as we have already seen and shall see below again.

Mundell's model should be thought of as a textbook model which imparts many useful insights but remains an over-simplification. One major criticism that has been levelled at it is that the capital flow equation is inconsistent with portfolio theory, which focuses on the demand for stocks. In the presence of uncertainty, an interest rate change will lead to a once-and-for-all adjustment of portfolios rather than a perpetual flow. However, at least the Mundell approach did include a monetary sector and as such was the first step in the evolution of a major critique of Keynesian balance of payments theory.

The Monetary Approach to the Balance of Payments

It has been seen that Keynesian balance of payments theory concentrates on the market for goods. The principal effect of an exogenous increase in exports in the expenditure model would be to change income through the multiplier process. It was not always thus. In the classical world of David Hume trade deficits were associated directly with money supply changes.

Consider a pure gold standard world in which gold is both the internal and the external money. If the domestic economy developed a balance of payments surplus, a classical economist would point to the fact that the domestic gold stock would be rising by the amount of the surplus *per period*. In other words, any imbalance in the value of goods flows is matched by net money flows in the opposite direction. The adjustment process from here on would be automatic since the rise in the domestic money stock would raise domestic money prices and cause a substitution of foreign for domestic goods. Thus the balance of payment surplus would disappear. This is the price-specie flow mechanism of classical economics.

Notice that where the internal and external money is the same the balance of payments is not a problem *per se*. Outflows of bullion may have caused banking crises and contraction of the money stock may have caused unemployment, but the balance of payments was no more a problem in the pure gold standard world than the balance of payments of East Anglia is today. There was, of course, a problem when paper backed by gold began to circulate as money, because external payments required bullion. As a result, the reserve ratios of banks came under pressure whenever gold left the country. However, this was not an 'official sector' problem as reserve outflows under fixed exchange rates would be today. In the modern world, where each nation state has its own fiat money, it might be thought that there has ceased to be a connection between the domestic money stock and the balance of payments. However, this is not true if the authorities are intervening to support the domestic exchange rate.

The process of pegging an exchange rate means that, in the UK case, the Bank of England takes up the residual excess demand or supply of foreign exchange at or close to the pegged price. If the UK had a balance of payments surplus, the authorities would buy foreign exchange with newly issued sterling. The foreign money would go into reserves and the sterling would go into the domestic money supply so long as it is spent on UK goods. The new increase in the money supply could be 'sterilised' by open market bond sales but this is of limited use since the process of selling more government debt would raise domestic interest rates and thereby induce additional capital inflows which would increase the balance of payments surplus still further.

The monetary approach points out that since the balance of payments has monetary effects, and is indeed a monetary 'problem', the domestic demand for money (or indeed other assets) should be an integral part of balance of payments analysis. If money continues to flow across the international exchanges then domestic money markets cannot be in equilibrium. An excess supply of money domestically will be reflected in an outlow across the exchanges. As the absorption approach emphasised, the balance of payments on current account is by definition equal to the difference between what the economy earns (output) and what it spends (national expenditure). Any group or individual for whom income and spending differ will be changing asset holdings. The decisions to spend or save are the opposite sides of the same coin. However, specifying asset choices and expenditure decisions simultaneously offers insights which suppression of one or the other negates. The recent wave of literature on the monetary approach has restored the balance, though it is important not to tip too far in the opposite direction. Monetary factors are important but not to the exclusion of all else.

The most influential single contribution to the monetary approach is that of Johnson (1976). He considers a highly simplified world in which there are rigidly fixed exchange rates and all goods are traded at a single world price. Real income growth is exogenous. The domestic money demand function is given by:

7.3 $\qquad M_d = p.f(Y,r)$

> Real money demand depends upon real income and the rate of interest.

And the money supply is given by definition as the sum of money domestically created and money associated with international reserve changes.

7.4 $\qquad M_s = R + D$

> Money stock is equal to reserves plus domestic credit

If the system is in static equilibrium money demand will equal money supply and there will be no reserve changes. If, however, domestic income is perpetually growing, with constant world prices and interest rates, Johnson shows that the growth in reserves will be *positively* related to domestic income growth and *negatively* related to domestic credit expansion.

7.5 $\qquad g_R = \alpha_0 \eta_y g_y - \alpha_1 g_D$

where g_R, g_y and g_D are the growth rates of reserves, income and domestic credit respectively, and η_y is the income elasticity of demand for money.

This is a remarkable conclusion which implies that real income growth *alone* improves the balance of payments and is in stark contrast to the Keynesian model above, where a rise in income has exactly the opposite effect. How does this result come about? Very simply, if there is real income growth, at constant price and interest rate levels, then there will be growing demand for money for transactions purposes. An excess demand for money can be met in one of two ways, either through domestic credit creation or through a balance of payments surplus. If there is no domestic credit expansion, reserves will grow in line with the growth in money demand. The existence of an excess demand for money means that people will be spending less than their income. For the country as a whole there will be a balance of payments surplus. If, on the other hand, domestic credit expands faster than money demand, then there will be a loss of reserves through a balance of payments deficit. The problem, then, which causes balance of payments deficits and associated reserve losses is not income expansion itself but rather the authorities' policies designed to achieve expansion, which typically lead to excessive domestic credit expansion, possibly through overlarge budget deficits.

The monetary approach under fixed exchange rates should probably be thought of as a theory of reserve changes rather than the balance of payments, since it is not clear from the literature whether the effects will appear in the current or capital account. However, it should be obvious that many of the simplifying assumptions in the Johnson model are not at all critical. Indeed a wide range of possible macroeconomic models will have the above properties so long as they include a monetary sector and especially transactions demand for money.

The monetary approach does, however, resolve for us the apparent paradox of fast growing countries which appear to have perpetual balance of payments surpluses, though it does not tell us where this growth comes from. Indeed this approach predicts exactly this outcome, so long as the domestic monetary authority restricts the growth of domestic credit to less than the growth in money demand. Thus in countries like West Germany, since the fast growth in real income causes a growth in transactions demand for money, the economy induces an inflow of money via the foreign balance to the extent that this money is not created by the Central Bank. Since the economy is trying to acquire financial assets it will be spending less than the value of its output which is identical to running a balance of payments surplus. This surplus can be perpetual because growing income requires ever-growing money balances. The UK problem is the opposite — slow real growth and faster domestic credit expansion leading to perpetual balance of payments problems.

New Cambridge and New New Cambridge

The original analytical basis of the New Cambridge approach to the balance of payments has already been outlined in Chapter 6. Basically, the domestic economy has two sectors, private and government, and there is the overseas sector. If the private sector typically runs a small and stable (or even fairly small and predictable) surplus then it must be the case that an overall deficit for the economy as a whole is caused by a deficit in the government sector. The proposition is fairly obvious when seen in terms of the accounting identity

7.6 $\quad I + G + X \equiv S + T + P$

INJECTIONS $\equiv$ WITHDRAWALS

so

$$(S{-}I) \; + \; (T{-}G) \; + \; (P{-}X) \;\; \equiv 0$$

$$(T{-}G) + \; (S{-}I) \;\; \equiv \;\; (X{-}P)$$

If $(S{-}I)$, private sector net acquisition of financial assets, is small and approximately constant then $(T{-}G)$, the budget deficit, will determine changes in $(X{-}P)$, the balance of payments. Hence we get the view, once characteristic of New Cambridge, that the budget deficit determines the balance of payments.

This is a perfectly valid way to approach the balance of payments; however, it is based upon a dubious empirical proposition, as we have seen before in Chapter 6. Indeed, by appending a simple monetary sector to the model it is not hard to see that the New Cambridge story is just a highly special case of the monetary approach. Consider a world in which there is no growth and the demand for money is strictly proportional to national income (the Cambridge equation of Chapter 5). Suppose also that a government budget deficit is financed in such a way that it leads, *within the current year*, to an equal expansion of domestic credit. Now we make the further strong assumption that any excess supply of money is run down within the current year then, in the absence of a capital account, we get the New Cambridge result that the budget deficit matches the current account deficit. In the presence of a capital account we get the result that the budget deficit matches the overall balance of payments deficit (current plus capital account = reserve changes). Opponents of the monetary approach have, however, stressed that, since domestic money holdings may be in disequilibrium for some time, the approach is at best a long-run story. Paradoxically, New Cambridge have stressed the short-run nature of their approach. Someone must be wrong.

If New Cambridge had stuck to their guns it would seem that they should have been recommending very 'Monetarist' solutions to Britain's recent problem of a large balance of payments deficit and high inflation, i.e. elimination of the fiscal deficit. However, it would seem that their political affiliations would not allow this logic to hold, so another way out had to be found which gave priority to the unemployment target. Thus they came to the view that '. . . there seems now to be no way of obtaining simultaneously an improvement in the current balance and keeping unemployment below one million other than by introducing some form of import restriction' (*Economic Policy Review*, February 1975, No.1, p.3).

Import restrictions are the only policy New Cambridge could have come up with in the circumstances which would have avoided the label 'right wing.' The problem with import controls is that they are like trying to cure smallpox by putting plasters on the spots; one is attacking the symptoms rather than the cause itself. A balance of payments deficit arises when domestic expenditure exceeds domestic output. Import controls do nothing to change that. If domestic citizens are forced to buy fewer foreign goods they will buy more domestic goods which may otherwise have been exported. Only if the restricted imports are replaced by an increase in production of domestic substitutes can import controls work.

Fetherston and Godley (1978) have recently tried to demonstrate the benefits of import controls by simulating their effect in their model. However, it is worth recording Blinder's comments on this to show that the case is far from convincing:

> ... I should say something about the authors' comparative static experiment with what they call an 'import quota.' This generated a great deal of acrimonious comment at the conference as people wondered how import quotas could permanently raise real output while having no effect on the price level. How can the effects of tariffs and quotas be so different?
>
> The problem stems entirely from a misuse of language by the authors. They do *not* simulate the effect of an import quota at all ... Instead, what they *do* simulate is an autonomous downward shift in the import function. By plugging up some of the 'leakage' from the circular flow, this change naturally raises national income. Further, since prices are independent of demand, this demand stimulus does not move the price level. Finally, there is no way to capture the efficiency losses from import quotas within the context of a one-sector macro model like this one. Once all this is understood, there is no mystery about why 'import quotas' look like such a good policy; they are not import quotas at all. (Blinder 1978.)

Far from retreat from the idea of import controls as the UK balance of payments position has improved, the New Cambridge group, in the 1979 *Economic Policy Review*, goes so far as to propose them on a global scale. How import controls in a number of countries, including the US (which is the largest world market), can be thought of as a solution to a depression in world trade is beyond the comprehension of the author. The solution, we are told, does have a favourable outcome when simulated on a global version of the New Cambridge model, though by now the reader should have understood enough to treat the output of New Cambridge models with a great deal of scepticism (see, for example, Brittan 1979.)

Endogenous Exchange Rates

Much of the above discussion has presumed the existence of

fixed exchange rates. The widespread variability of exchange rates since 1971 has required a great deal more attention to be paid to flexible exchange rates and their policy implications. In the Keynesian type models the exchange rate is still treated as an exogenous variable which has two effects. The first effect is that, in so far as it changes the terms of trade or competitiveness, it causes changes in imports and exports. Secondly, a fall in the exchange rate *causes* inflation through the import cost component of prices, as in equation 2.14.

An endogenous treatment of the exchange rate, of course, requires an explicit model of the markets in which it is determined—the international money markets. Indeed HMT has now been extended to give the facility of integrating money and capital flows sectors with the national income forecasting model to provide a 'float run.' However, this development takes it beyond the bounds of the British Keynesian tradition and makes the Treasury a leader in the field — at least in the UK. The intellectual influences which have brought about this welcome integration have undoubtedly come from the monetary approach as applied to floating exchange rates. A collection of recent work in this area is provided in Frenkel and Johnson (1978).

The conventional textbook analysis of the exchange rate derives certain propositions about the *flow* demand for foreign exchange from the demands for imports and exports. Suppose there are two countries , the UK and the US. There is trade in goods between them. Each has a different domestic currency and the domestic currency price of domestic output is assumed to be fixed. The UK demands US goods but the sterling price in the UK depends upon how much UK citizens have to pay for dollars. The higher the price of dollars, the more expensive will be US goods in the UK, and vice versa. UK citizens demand a flow of dollars to pay for their imports and US citizens demand a flow of sterling to pay for UK exports.

In figure 7.3 the vertical axis shows the price of $1 in pounds, so going up the axis is devaluing the pound. The horizontal axis shows the quantity of dollars demanded or supplied in exchange for pounds. As the price of dollars rises UK citizens find the price of US goods has gone up, so they buy

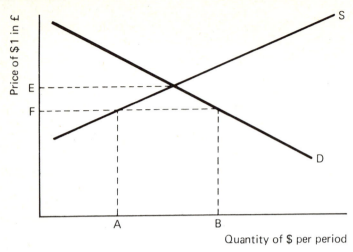

Figure 7.3

less of them. If demand is elastic they will buy both a smaller quantity and a *smaller value* and will, therefore, demand fewer dollars. In that case the demand curve for dollars D will be downward sloping with respect to the exchange rate. Even if the underlying demand curve for goods were negatively sloped, the demand curve for dollars would be upward sloping if the demand for goods were not elastic.

The supply of dollars, S, is upward sloping so long as US demand for UK goods is elastic, since they will buy a greater value of British goods as the pound is devalued. This is basically the elasticity approach to the balance of payments and it leads to the Marshall–Lerner condition. This is that for a devaluation to improve the balance of payments, the sum of the elasticities of demand for imports and exports must exceed one in absolute value. This is really the stability condition for the market depicted in figure 7.3, since if D were upward sloping and S downward sloping the market would be unstable in the sense that there would be excess demand above the equilibrium price and excess supply below.

This model is extremely helpful in illustrating why the balance of payments is such a problem when the authorities are trying to peg the exchange rate in an overvalued position, such as at F. Here there is an excess demand for dollars, which in this model is the same as a current account deficit, equal to $B-A$. The only way that the price F can be maintained is by the domestic authorities providing $B-A$ dollars per period out of reserves by, in effect, buying back sterling of equivalent value. Reserves are finite so this position is not sustainable indefinitely. A short-term solution is to borrow more reserves and give those away as well. A devaluation would involve changing the intervention price to E. But the conventional response in the 1950s and early 1960s was to depress domestic expenditures so that the D curve would be shifted to the left.

The monetary approach is critical of treating exchange rates as solely determined by flow demand for currencies derived from flow demands for goods. Exchange rates are the relative price of two moneys, so surely conditions in money markets must have some part to play. In a world of mobile financial capital the critical condition to be met is that all money stocks and financial asset stocks must be willingly held, at the margin. If there are excess money supplies or portfolio disequilibria, then financial capital will be flowing internationally and, in the absence of central bank intervention, exchange rates will be changing.

The principal difference between the fixed and floating exchange rate cases of the monetary approach is that, in the former, the price level was fixed to that of the rest of the world and the nominal money supply could change through induced reserve changes. In the latter there are no reserve changes and the nominal domestic money supply is fixed by the authorities. However, the *real* money supply is determined endogenously because domestic currency prices are no longer tied to foreign prices. Monetary expansion by the authorities now leads to downward pressure on the exchange rate and upward pressure on the domestic price level. The exchange rate measures the value of domestic money in terms of other moneys. The price level measures the value of domestic money in terms of goods. They are both indicators of the same thing — declining value of the domestic money. Neither is the cause of inflation, both are different aspects of the same inflation. This is not to deny that inflationary experience will be different if some inflation is 'bought back' by running down reserves, as compared to allowing the exchange rate to float.

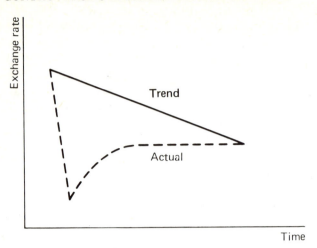

Figure 7.4

The monetary approach to the exchange rate does not claim that only monetary factors are important, but it does stress the importance of money markets in the short-run determination of exchange rates. This is because it may take a long time for price changes to influence goods markets, but the international 'wholesale' money markets are highly sensitive to minute interest differentials and expected exchange rate changes. If these markets anticipate an exchange rate change as a result of, say, some policy change, holders will tend to move immediately out of the currency which is expected to decline in value. While there is a movement out of a currency the exchange rate will tend to overshoot and later return once the adjustment has taken place, as in figure 7.4. Floating currencies do not move smoothly in line with inflation differentials. They adjust quickly to new information but with a tendency to overshoot. Considerable empirical work remains to be done in this area as data become available for longer periods.

Finally, it is important to avoid confusion about whether the monetary approach is a long-run or short-run theory. The fixed rate case was criticised by some for only explaining the long-run situation, while the proponents of the floating case espouse it as providing the dominant short-run explanation of

exchange rates. It would seem that the behaviour of the exogenous authorities can change a model from long-run to short-
run or vice versa. The answer to this paradox is very simple.
In both cases transactions demand for money for most individuals and non-financial firms can be out of equilibrium for
long periods. International goods arbitrage is also slow, so
that the 'law of one price' or purchasing power parity are at
best long-run equilibrium conditions. However, interest arbitrage equilibrium conditions as between financial firms such as
international banks hold almost exactly even in the very
short run. Homo economicus is alive and well and making a
living off fractions of one percentage point in the international
money markets. The monetary approach *in both fixed and
floating exchange rate cases* is a theory of short-run international portfolio adjustments, i.e. capital flows. These
markets adjust most quickly and can thus dominate exchange
markets in the short run. They are thus vital components to
the explanation of short-run exchange rate changes in one
case and reserve changes in the other. In the long run wider
influences come into play.

Balance of Payments — A Problem for Whom?

The above analysis has presented no simple view of what it
is about the balance of payments that is problematic. Why
should we worry if the balance of payments is in deficit?
The answer is that the balance of payments of the UK should
be of little more importance to any citizen of the UK than the
balance of payments of Manchester is to a Mancunian. Con-
suming more than one's income is not a particularly painful
experience, though it cannot be sustained indefinitely. If,
however, one lives in an area which does have a balance of
payments deficit for a long period, its wealth will be declining
and it will eventually become a depressed area.

It is not normally the depressing effects of balance of payments deficits which make the balance of payments a pressing
and immediate political problem. Rather this occurs when
the authorities are (or feel) committed to maintaining a pegged
value of the exchange rate. Then it is the inadequacy of

Central Bank reserves which is the problem. The authorities cannot fail to be aware of a balance of payments deficit in these circumstances because they know how many reserves they are losing minute by minute. Millions unemployed or rapid inflation are not nearly so impressive in the psyche of a Governor of the Bank of England as a major loss of reserves, even though it should now be clear that a major reserve loss is most likely to be caused by the authorities' own domestic monetary policies.

The floating exchange rate equivalent of a reserve loss is currency depreciation. Any sustained downward trend in the value of a currency is likely to be in response to expansionary monetary and fiscal policies, though depreciation of a currency is much less of a direct problem for the authorities than is a loss of reserves. The floating exchange rate dual of reserve losses is inflation which is felt by the general population and not primarily by the Central Bank. To this question we now turn.

Summary

The balance of payments is not a single unambiguous entity nor is it always an immediate problem. Different ways of modelling the economy necessarily give different views of the issue. One thing that is clear, however, is that the way in which the balance of payments encroaches upon the domestic economy depends critically upon the structure and behaviour of the monetary institutions. A floating exchange rate operates in a very different way from a fixed exchange rate and models which do not recognise this fact miss a great deal.

In an open economy like the UK, external influences are obviously very large and it is important that we should try to understand them. Much progress has been made in the last decade, but a great deal more work remains to be done.

8

Inflation and Unemployment

*I hold that if the Almighty had ever made a set of
men that should do all the eating and none of the
work, He would have made them with mouths only and
no hands; and if He had ever made another class
that He intended should do all the work and no
eating, He would have made them with hands only
and no mouths.*
LINCOLN

Inflation is a sustained rise in the money price index of all
goods and services, or, equivalently, a sustained decline in the
value of money. Between 1951 and 1967 the rate of inflation
in the UK never exceeded 6% per annum. In 1975 it reached
a peak of the order of 25% per annum. It is not surprising
that the problem of inflation has dominated policy discussions
during the 1970s. What is surprising is the large amount of
disagreement that remains about how the recent economic
history of the UK should be interpreted. The Monetarists are
convinced that excessive aggregate monetary expenditure is
to blame, whereas Keynesians seem convinced that the blame
should be laid at the feet of cost-push influences — primarily
the trade unions and the oil producers. The evidence that will
be presented seems to be more supportive of the former than
the latter.

As we have seen in earlier chapters, the price level is not
an endogenous variable in simple Keynesian models. Model II
permits the price level to be endogenous but at the expense
of fixing the level of employment. Later in this chapter an
analytic outline of recent events will be presented in the
context of Model III. Before this, however, it is convenient
to discuss a number of other influential analytical approaches.

The Accounting or Forecasting Approach

It was shown in Chapter 2 that the price level has typically been forecast in the UK by extrapolating cost changes which are either known or assumed to have occurred. This is based on the identity that price per unit output (p.u.o.) must be equal to wages p.u.o. plus profits p.u.o. plus raw material costs p.u.o. plus indirect taxes p.u.o. The forecasters usually assume profits p.u.o. to be constant and obtain fairly accurate short-term forecasts by including import prices for raw material costs. The short-term accuracy of this method is guaranteed by the fact that relevant cost changes have already happened, so it is safe to predict that eventually they will work through to goods prices. However, one must be careful not to read too much of substance into this approach, because an identity which must be true *whatever the cause of inflation* is often erroneously given the status of a theory which says that inflation is *caused* by changes in these components of output prices. For example, G.D.N. Worswick, the Director of the National Institute, said in his evidence to the Public Expenditure Committee (p. 38):

> The factors determining the movement of prices in this country are many. The principal ones are the level of wages and costs. The secondary one is profit margins. In some countries you get a profit-generated inflation. I do not think this has happened in the UK. Thirdly, there is the intervention by government by taxes or subsidies to raise or lower the market price from the factor cost price. Fourthly, there is the import cost.

The danger of this approach is that it points to direct controls over wages and profits as being the only way to cure inflation, since this is where inflation starts. Even more absurd is that it makes it appear that reductions in indirect taxes, which in Keynesian terms would be an *injection* into the circular flow, are actually disinflationary. After all, as Mr Worswick continued, 'If the position is affected by four variables, it is necessary to control as many of them as you can.' If you still have inflation after all that, you can put the blame on foreigners! Small wonder we found the Chancellor, in 1976 and 1977, offering tax reductions as a bribe to the unions to accept an incomes policy.

Unemployment, in Chapter 2, had no direct relationship with inflation for periods of incomes policies. The unemployment forecasts depended upon a productivity trend, the level of output and demographic factors affecting the size of the labour force. Unemployment therefore was not judged to be important in determining inflation during quite long periods and formerly the reverse would have been true. The 1978 version of HMT does, however, have an indirect effect running from inflation to unemployment. This arises because a rise in the price level now reduces the level of consumption expenditure. There is also now an indirect effect of unemployment upon output because of its effect of raising precautionary saving. To a large extent, however, it is fair to record that the Treasury forecasters do not treat inflation and unemployment as closely related phenomena, even though they do have unemployment in the 'earnings' equation in addition to these other feedbacks.

The Phillips Curve

One of the most famous relationships in macroeconomics is the inverse relationship between inflation and unemployment identified by A.W. Phillips (1958) and hence known as the Phillips curve. This relationship was, however, pointed out much earlier in the USA by Irving Fisher (1926). Further important supportive work on the Phillips curve was done by Lipsey (1960).

The problem Phillips posed for himself was how to explain the dynamic behaviour of a macro-model such as Model II when it was close to full employment. The textbook models had only real output changing at less than full employment, whereas at full employment only prices changed. Phillips focused particularly on the labour market and proposed that as the pressure of demand, as measured by unemployment, got greater and greater, the rate of increase of wages would rise. As a zero level of unemployment was approached the rate of increase of wages would approach infinity. Phillips showed that the evidence of nearly 100 years was consistent with the existence of a stable relationship as depicted in figure 8.1. The

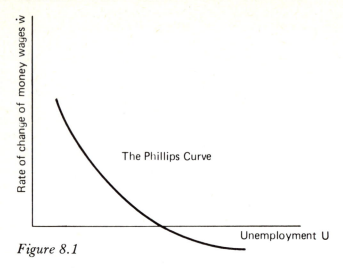

Figure 8.1

theoretical underpinnings were refined by Lipsey who worked in terms of separate wage and price equations. Wages were determined by unemployment, and prices were determined by a markup on wages plus other costs (in a similar manner to the forecasting equation 2.14). Followers often dropped this refinement and simply drew figure 8.1 with inflation, $\dot{p}$, on the vertical axis instead of $\dot{w}$. It is now a commonplace to draw the Phillips curve as a relationship between $\dot{p}$ and U, and this practice will be continued below.

The Phillips curve was widely adopted by economists in the early 1960s as filling in a gap in the standard version of Model II. During this period it was generally accepted that inflation was mainly caused by demand factors, though even Phillips was fully aware that cost factors, especially import prices, *could* exert an independent influence on the price level. However, they had not often done so in the previous 100 years. The only serious support for the view that internal cost pressures could exert upward pressure on prices, independent of the level of demand, was offered by Hines (1964). Hines used the rate of change of union membership as an index of union pushfulness and claimed that this offered a significant improvement in the explanation of wage changes. Purdy and Zis (1973), however, provided a comprehensive critique of Hines' results.

After devaluation in 1967, of course, the inflationary experience was considerably worse than previously, as Phillips himself would have predicted. Wages, however, lagged behind prices owing to the incomes policy of 1968—9 and also presumably because people did not know what to expect in terms of price rises. The resultant 'wage explosion' in 1969 was widely interpreted as proving the possibility of wage push independent of the level of demand. However, it can also be interpreted as a catch up of expectations to reality as we shall see below. Laidler (1976) argues that over this period the country was merely reimporting the inflation it had previously been exporting.

Even if the data from the late 1960s could be made to fit with the simple Phillips curve, the data from the 1970s certainly could not. Indeed, the theoretical basis of the simple Phillips curve had been undermined independently by Phelps (1967) and Friedman (1968) long before events had made this reappraisal necessary. The Phelps—Friedman approach forms the basis of the model to be developed below.

An essential ingredient of the modified approach to the Phillips curve is the idea that unions bargain for real wages rather than nominal wages. Thus the Phillips curve has to be shifted up for each level of expected inflation. There is then a short-run trade off between inflation and unemployment for each *given* expected rate of inflation. Several economists in the UK, however, have tried to drop the idea of a short-run Phillips curve and take the real wage target as the exogenous factor which drives inflation almost alone, and which is certainly not affected by the level of employment in an inverse direction. This approach will be discussed below.

Aggregate Demand and Supply

The major split over inflation is often characterised as being between those who think it comes basically from aggregate demand and those who think it comes from the supply side of the economy. Most would agree that an expansion of the money stock is necessary to sustain a price level rise but those who believe in cost-push usually argue that the money

stock has to be expanded in the wake of inflation to avoid
unemployment. Both lines of argument could be valid. The
question is, what actually happened in any particular episode?

Let us first look at the price level and the level of output
in terms of Model III. Following Gordon (1978) it is convenient to combine the two versions of Model III by a simple
modification of the aggregate supply curve. For the short-run
case where money illusion was assumed on the part of suppliers
of labour, we assume that labour supply depends upon the
expected price level p^e. Demand for labour on the other hand
depends upon the actual price level. In the short run, while
expectations lag behind reality, the aggregate supply curve
will be upward sloping but it will shift leftward if expectations
are revised upwards. In the long run expectations are correct
so the long-run supply curve is vertical at the trend output
level — sometimes called the 'natural' output level. In other
words, the long-run supply curve shifts rightwards each period
because of the underlying growth of the economy.

If we consider the initial position in figure 8.2 to be at
point A then it is clear that a price level rise can be started by
either a rightward shift of aggregate demand D_1 or a leftward
shift of aggregate supply. A cost-induced inflation would

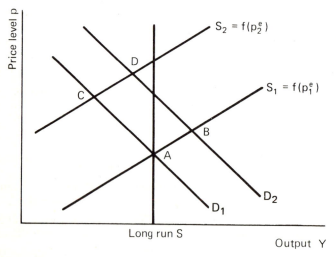

Figure 8.2

involve a supply side shift and the economy would move from A to C. A move to D would then follow if measures were taken to eliminate unemployment. Eventually the system would settle again at a higher price level on the long-run aggregate supply curve. A demand-induced inflation, however, would be caused by a shift of the demand curve to, say, D_2 so the economy would move from A to B. Expectations would then be revised so that S_1 would shift in the direction of S_2 and the economy would move to a point like D. Whether D is in this case to the left or right of long-run S does not matter — either is possible. The point is that a demand-induced inflation will move the economy through an anticlockwise arc initially. A supply-induced inflation will move it through a clockwise arc.

The picture in the UK is extremely clear, as figure 8.3 shows, so long as it is appropriate to start the cycle in 1971. The end of 1971 marks the beginning of a major expansion of the money supply associated with competition and credit control, and March 1972 was the date of Mr Barber's famous expansionary budget. Hence a shift of demand moves the economy along a short-run supply curve, which incidentally appears to be fairly flat. From 1973 to 1975 it looks very much as if a leftward shift of the aggregate supply curve is moving the economy back up the aggregate demand curve, which is fairly steep. 1976 is almost due north of 1975, so there seems to be some reflation here plus a further shift left of the supply curve.

Notice that while the movement from 1973 to 1975 must involve a shift of the supply curve some such shift would be an essential part of the demand-induced story. The economy cannot stay at a point like B in figure 8.2 because it is beyond the long-run supply curve. Price expectations will necessarily shift the supply curve leftward sooner or later. It is quite likely that the oil price rise increased the shift of supply between 1973 and 1975, but it is important to realise that after the events of 1971–3 some such shift would have occurred anyway due to the behaviour of expectations.

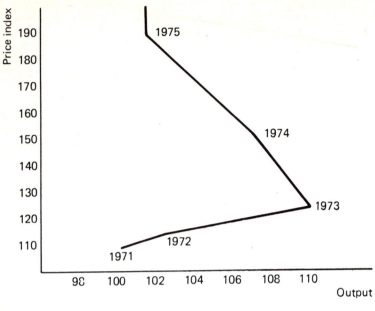

1970 = 100

	Price index all manufactured products	Output all industries
1971	109	100.3
1972	114.8	102.5
1973	123.2	109.9
1974	152	106.9
1975	183.7	101.5
1976	219.6	102

Figure 8.3 (Source: NIESR)

The Expectations Augmented Phillips Curve

The above analysis is couched in terms of the price level and the level of output. An analogous argument can be developed in the more familiar dimensions of inflation and unemployment. It was seen above that a single stable Phillips curve is incapable of reconciling the observation of both high inflation and high unemployment. Once, however, it is admitted that

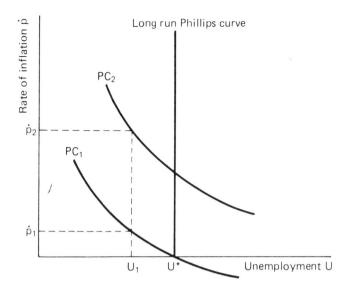

Figure 8.4

there is a new higher Phillips curve for each higher expected rate of inflation events become easy to explain.

Suppose curve PC_1 in figure 8.4 is the Phillips curve for zero expected inflation. If the level of unemployment is U^*, this expectation will be fulfilled and nothing need change. However, if unemployment were U_1 inflation would be greater than zero at $\dot{p}_1$. Next period expectations would be revised upwards so there would be a higher Phillips curve, say PC_2, so again inflation would be higher than expected and, so long as unemployment stayed at U_1, inflation would accelerate. This is sometimes called the 'accelerationist' hypothesis as a result. The long-run Phillips curve traces out the point on each Phillips curve at which expectations will be fulfilled, so they are points of stable inflation. If the long-run is defined as the period within which expectations are fulfilled, then the long-run Phillips curve is vertical *by definition*, though for other definitions of 'long-run' the long-run Phillips curve may be negatively sloped. The point on which it stands on the unemployment axis is known as the 'natural' rate of unemployment. This is thus exogenous to the inflation process but can be influenced by structural changes in the economy.

In order to explain what happens to the course of inflation and unemployment in reality it is necessary to add to this picture some statement about the growth of aggregate demand. There are really two separate relationships that can be identified between aggregate demand growth and inflation/ unemployment. These are illustrated in figure 8.5. Let us assume for simplicity that there is no productivity growth, so that output is constant at the 'natural' level of unemployment. Whatever the rate of growth of aggregate monetary demand happens to be determines the long-run budget constraint of the economy. This tells us that the inflation rate (at a constant 'natural' output level) will be equal to the growth rate of aggregate demand. If aggregate demand in money terms is growing at 10% per annum the long-run budget constraint will be a horizontal line at a 10% inflation rate (or lower if the productivity assumption is changed).

The other relationship is that *for each period* we have a short-run budget constraint SBC. This is derived from the fact that within any period the rate of growth of nominal domestic expenditure must be equal to the rate of growth of real output plus the rate of inflation. This means that for any *given* rate of growth of nominal demand there is an inverse relationship between inflation and real output growth. The higher the inflation rate the lower will be the real growth rate and vice versa. If, in addition, we presume the existence of a relationship known as Okun's Law, which in essence means that higher output (relative to trend) is associated with lower unemployment, we then get the short-run budget constraint which expresses the fact that *for a given growth-rate of demand* higher inflation will be associated with higher unemployment (because it is associated with lower output).

Whereas the long-run budget constraint is fixed by the exogenously determined growth in demand, the short-run budget constraint shifts whenever the actual inflation rate differs from its long-run level. This is because its intersection with the long-run budget constraint is determined by the previous period's level of output (and therefore of unemployment). This is the base for next period's growth. So SBC

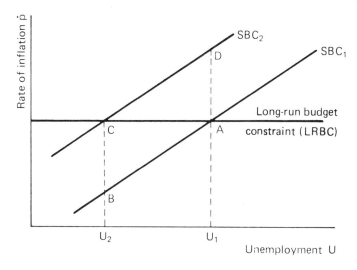

Figure 8.5 Budget constraints

always intersects the long-run budget constraint at last period's level of unemployment. For example, if in figure 8.5 we start at point A, unemployment now falls from U_1 to U_2, so the current outcome is at B. Next period, the budget constraint will intersect LRBC at C. If now for some reason inflation rises to the level at D, unemployment will rise to U_1 this period and next period SBC will again intersect LRBC at A. We now need to combine the budget constraints with the Phillips curves to analyse the inflation process.

Consider the course of inflation and unemployment that would occur if the economy were initially at the natural level of unemployment with zero inflation and zero growth of aggregate nominal demand. Now the growth rate of aggregate demand is raised to 10%. What happens? The long-run budget constraint becomes a horizontal line at the inflation rate of 10%, as depicted in figure 8.6. The new short-run budget constraint SBC_2 passes through the long-run budget constraint at the initial level of unemployment, i.e. at G. The short-run Phillips curve is PC_1 so the economy moves from the initial position $(U^*, \dot{p}=0)$ to A. Next period, the new short-run budget constraint will be SBC_3 and, if the short-run Phillips curve did not shift, the economy would go to B and

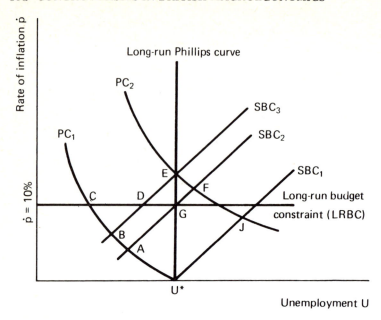

Figure 8.6

then converge on C. However, expected inflation will now start to shift the short-run Phillips curve up to the right. If it now intersects SBC_3 at D the budget constraint will stay put for one period but the short-run Phillips curve will continue to move to the right.

Once the intersection of PC and SBC is *above* the long-run budget constraint, the SBC curve will now start to shift back down to the right. And once the economy is *to the right* of the long-run Phillips curve, the PC curve will start to shift back down to the left. Thus from a point such as E which is on PC_2 and SBC_3 we move to F on PC_2 and SBC_2. From F both the SBC curve and the PC curve will shift down, so the next position could well be southeast of G. Clearly, the economy will home into the long-run equilibrium point G in a clockwise cycle, presuming, that is, that the expectations feedback is reasonably stable, so that the economy does not explode.

It is important to notice that, while we have conducted the simplest possible experiment of raising demand growth from

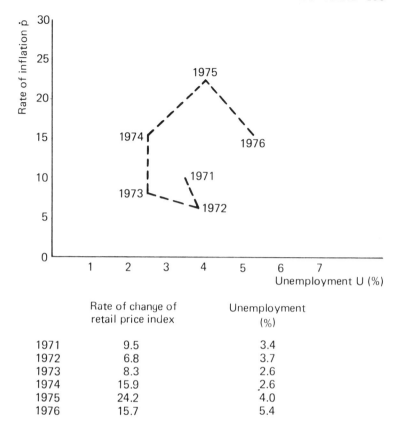

	Rate of change of retail price index	Unemployment (%)
1971	9.5	3.4
1972	6.8	3.7
1973	8.3	2.6
1974	15.9	2.6
1975	24.2	4.0
1976	15.7	5.4

Figure 8.7 (Source: NIESR)

zero to 10%, we have discovered a pattern of response which includes periods of rising inflation and rising unemployment, falling inflation and rising unemployment, as well as rising inflation and falling unemployment. The economy has moved through a clockwise convergent cycle from the initial position through A, D, E and F, and eventually to G.

Figure 8.7 plots the actual course of the UK economy during its most recent inflation cycle. The movement from 1971 to 1972 can be regarded as the tail of the previous cycle. From 1972 there is a clear clockwise cycle which is entirely consistent with a demand-induced inflation as above. Specific factors such as the oil price rise and incomes policies will no doubt have an influence on the numerical size of various shifts. But it is hard to see how these specific factors could explain the pattern as a whole. For example, if the oil crisis had struck at the initial position in figure 8.6 and the authorities had maintained the level of domestic demand constant, the economy would initially have moved northeast to a point like J.

While the above explanation may be labelled 'monetarist' in the UK, it would certainly be embraced by both Monetarists and Keynesians in the US. Indeed, the above analysis is an exact analogue of that applied to the recent US experience by Gordon (1978, Chapter 8). It is hard to escape the parallels between Gordon's figure 8–11 (p.237) and figure 8.7 above. The US economy shows exactly the same clockwise cycle in the 1970s, though the inflation rates are considerably lower and the unemployment rates somewhat higher than in the UK. On the basis of figure 8.7, the natural rate of unemployment in the UK looks to be about 3%. Sumner (1978) reports that up to 1968 the natural rate of unemployment was 1.9%, while after 1968 it rose to 3.2%.

Inflation, Money and Exchange Rates

It is difficult to do justice to the topic of inflation in one short chapter in a short book. However, it is impossible to pass on without saying something more about the role of money in inflation and also about the influence of the exchange rate regime.

It should be abundantly clear by now that very few Monetarists would now claim that money is the *only* thing that needs to be looked at in explaining inflation. Indeed, it is the Monetarists who have been most concerned to incorporate supply side dynamics into the story. Most Monetarists would surely have to agree that price level rises could be caused, in the framework of figure 8.2, by anything that shifts either the aggregate supply curve or the aggregate demand curve. However, shifts on the supply side caused by, say, a bad harvest and on the demand side caused by, say, fiscal policy are likely to provide at most a *once and for all*

rise in the price level. Only monetary expansion is uncon-
strained and is thus the most likely candidate for causing
sustained periods of inflation. Indeed, it is almost impossible
to find significant examples of inflation which are not
associated with monetary expansion. This is what Friedman
meant by the famous statement that 'Inflation is always and
everywhere a monetary phenomenon'.

Another important point to notice is that the correct *level*
at which to analyse inflation may not be that of the individual
nation state. One man's output price is another man's cost.
What may seem like cost inflation through import prices in
the UK may in fact be caused by over-expansion of global
aggregate demand, of which UK demand is only a very small
part. The blame for the recent upward trend in world inflation
has been attributed by some to expansionary policies in the
USA, associated with the Vietnam War. Those who point to
the importance of worldwide demand factors as a source of
worldwide inflation are sometimes labelled 'international
monetarists'.

For a small country, like the UK, in a big world the
thing to be explained is the deviation of the domestic inflation
rate from the world rate. In this regard the exchange rate
regime is absolutely central. If a country has a fixed exchange
rate it will reach a reserve crisis long before domestic inflation
exceeds external inflation by a dramatic amount. Indeed, the
very process of tying the value of domestic money to the
value of foreign money involves also tying the rate of exchange
between domestic money and *traded* goods. Only a country
with a flexible exchange rate could have experienced the high
levels of inflation depicted in figure 8.7, given that other
major countries had so much lower inflation rates. The excess
of inflation over the world rate is reflected in a depreciation
of the domestic currency. The two significant changes that
have happened in the economic environment since 1967 are
that exchange rates have become more variable and the world
inflation rate has risen. The UK experience must be seen in
that context.

Real Wage Resistance

Some commentators in the UK continue to believe that the driving force of UK inflation is an exogenous wage push. Popular among them is the idea that trade unions aim for a fixed rate of increase in real wages come hell or high water.

The New Cambridge model of inflation has already been discussed. Indeed, their model suggests that lower unemployment will reduce inflation because it increases the real wage bill and so reduces the money wage increase required to achieve the real wage target. Empirical support for the idea of a real wage target is offered by Henry *et al.* (1976) who first re-estimated other inflation models including those of Lipsey and Hines. All the old models appear to do badly, especially when adjusted for autocorrelated residuals. A model based on the idea of a target real wage appears to fit well but this is the only one not adjusted for autocorrelation. Henry *et al.* conclude that for their data period there had been a target rate of growth of real wages of the order of 2% per annum.

Although this result may be correctly estimated it is comforting to note that the real wage target grew at exactly the rate which the economy could afford to pay. It is well known that the trend growth rate of productivity is of this order of magnitude. Perhaps there is an identification problem here. Surely what is being estimated is the *actual* trend rate of growth of real wages not the target rate in the minds of unions. Other criticisms of Henry *et al.* are provided in Parkin (1978).

This issue is controversial and may not be settled for some years. All sides are now agreed that people bargain for real wages. Some see this as part of a broader dynamic picture which is influenced by the level of demand. Others, however, see the real wage target as either constant or, at least, as exogenous. It seems hard to believe that the level of unemployment has no influence whatsoever.

The Scandinavian or Nordic Model

One approach to the international transmission of inflation

is the Scandinavian model — so called because of its geographical origins (see Aukrust 1977 and Edgren, Faxen and Ohdner 1969). This should not be thought of as a complete picture of inflation. Rather it explains how an economy with a fixed exchange rate can have an inflation in excess of the world rate without necessarily incurring balance of payments problems. The other interesting aspect of this model is that it has two sectors, whereas the macro-model used above has only one sector.

One sector of the economy produces traded goods and is exposed to foreign competition. Since it sells its output in perfectly competitive markets it is a price-taker. Its prices are determined exogenously in world markets. This is true of both domestic and foreign currency prices because there is a fixed exchange rate. The other sector, which may be thought of as services, is not exposed to foreign competition and so has some discretion over prices. It has some degree of local monopoly power. Another important difference between the two sectors is that productivity is greater in the exposed sector than in the sheltered sector. This is because the service sector is more labour intensive than manufacturing industry.

The mechanism of the Scandinavian model is now quite simple. It starts with a price rise in world goods markets. This increases the prices and consequently the profits of the exposed sector. These increased profits are substantially passed on in the form of higher wages. Workers in the sheltered sector see these wages and bargain for a similar rise themselves. Being an egalitarian society, wage parity is maintained. However, because the sheltered sector is labour intensive, the price rises required in the sheltered sector in order to pay the higher wages are greater than the initial price rises in the exposed sector. Thus, because of wage equality and productivity differences, the net domestic inflation rate will exceed the inflation in export prices which triggered the process off. This is not a problem, however, so long as export prices remain competitive.

Aspects of the Scandinavian approach have been adopted by the London Business School modellers (see, for example, Ball and Burns 1976), but it should be clear that this approach has limited applicability to the UK at present. We do not have a fixed exchange rate, it is not clear to what extent our exporters are price-takers, and it is not known whether wage rises in export industries are imitated elsewhere. However, the two-sector model does provide insights which may well be helpful in understanding the UK experience.

Incomes Policies

Many books have been written both for and against incomes policies and no doubt many more are yet to come. We shall not devote a great deal of space to this issue because it does not relate directly to the structure of macro-models. However, it does seem worth pointing out that incomes policies are often viewed with scepticism by professional economists, both in the UK and elsewhere, even though they are often resorted to by UK politicians and are apparently so popular with the UK public.

The academic objection to incomes policy is usually based upon three propositions. The first is that *independent* wage-push is not the cause of inflation and so an incomes policy must eventually be frustrated because it does not tackle the root cause of the problem. This leads to the second point which is that while an incomes policy can have no long-run effect, it will work in holding down wages in some areas, and so there will be distortions introduced in the process of allocating labour. The economy will thus be less efficient. Finally, and perhaps strongest of all, is the point that it has proved extremely difficult to demonstrate that incomes policies have had any significant effect at all in the UK in the last 25 years. Parkin, Sumner and Jones (1972), for example, in their survey of the evidence on this subject, conclude that:

> ... On the basis of our present knowledge, it is possible to say that, with the exception of the immediate post-war experiment, incomes policy apparently has little effect either on the wage determination process or on the average rate of wage inflation ... (p. 13)

> ... The existing evidence indicates that incomes policies have had no identifiable effect on the price equation ... (p. 25)

How then might an incomes policy work in the context of the model in figure 8.6? It should be clear that the long-run position of the economy depends only upon the long-run budget constraint and upon the natural rate of unemployment. The long-run budget constraint depends entirely upon the policy-determined growth of monetary demand. So incomes policy could not influence the long-run inflation rate in this model. However, it could influence the short-run course of the economy *if and only if* it succeeds in lowering inflationary expectations. In this case the short-run Phillips curve would shift down to the left. For a given short-run budget constraint inflation would be lower and employment would be higher than otherwise. If this could be achieved, then, even if the long-run inflation rate were unchanged, a higher average level of output and lower average unemployment could be attained. This would undoubtedly be preferable to the situation in which there was no incomes policy.

The problem with an incomes policy is that even if the initial effect is favourable then the belief that the policy is ending can have an equal adverse effect or even worse. The expectation of the collapse of an incomes policy would shift the short-run Phillips curve up to the right, thus making inflation and unemployment worse. Many economists believe that this is exactly what happens. A short-run benefit is fairly quickly offset by an equal deterioration. Henry and Ormerod (1978), for example, conclude that:

> . . . Whilst some incomes policies have reduced the rate of wage inflation during the period in which they operated, this reduction has only been temporary. Wage increases in the period immediately following the ending of the policies were higher than they would otherwise have been, and these increases match losses incurred during the operation of the incomes policy. (p. 39)

Thus while it is logically possible that incomes policies could improve the dynamic path towards *any* long-run inflation rate, there is no evidence that they have done so in the recent past. Any short-run benefit in terms of higher employment and lower inflation is subsequently offset by higher inflation and lower employment as the policy breaks down.

There are two possible stories about this breakdown. The

first is the catching up of expectations that has been mentioned above. The second gives a critical role to the public sector. It is argued that incomes policies have their greatest impact on public sector wages since the government is in effect itself the employer, whereas private sector employers can get around the policy if market conditions demand. As time passes the public sector employees notice that their wages are falling behind comparable private sector groups and demand 'pay comparability'. This leads to substantial public sector 'catch up' awards which effectively herald the end of the incomes policy. In 1979 the Labour Government even went so far as to set up a Public Sector Comparability Commision to deal with the multiplicity of public sector groups who felt that they had suffered under successive phases of incomes policies.

This points to the existence of two separate problems in this area. The first is how to make incomes policies more widely effective and other than in the short run. The answer to this is that it is probably not worth trying, since the administrative and distortionary costs would seem to be prohibitive in peace time. The second problem is how to determine public sector wages. The larger is the public sector share of employment the more inappropriate it becomes to set public sector wages by comparison with the private sector. In the end there could be just one man left in the private sector whose wages determine those for the rest of the economy! A more coherent public sector wages policy is required which is made consistent with other aspects of policy such as employment and public expenditure targets and bears a sensible relationship to the underlying growth pattern of the real economy. Neither the adoption or abandonment of incomes policies obviates the need for a sensible policy towards public sector pay.

Summary

There is still wide disagreement about the causes of inflation in the UK and, therefore, also about appropriate cures. Some influential commentators in the Keynesian tradition still see inflation as caused by exogenous cost-push factors. It is argued here that, once the formation of inflation expectations is endogenised, a coherent analytical framework is available which appears to be consistent with the most recent major inflation cycle in the UK. The primary explanatory variable in this story is the behaviour of policy-determined aggregate demand (at both a domestic and world level). Important advances in our understanding of price and wage-setting behaviour in inflationary periods are at the heart of this modern economics of inflation. A survey of the recent UK work in this area is presented in Parkin (1978). Of almost equal importance to the understanding of UK inflation is the external environment. The level of (and causes of) world inflation and the exchange rate regime are critical elements in the explanation of the actual level of inflation experienced.

9

Crowding Out

And though each spring do add to love new heat,
As princes do in times of action get
New taxes, and remit them not in peace,
No winter shall abate the spring's increase.
DONNE

The issues over which there is still probably the greatest disagreement, both in North America and the UK, are those of crowding out and fine tuning. These are the subject of this chapter and the next. The central issue in both these topics is the role of government in the macroeconomy. As a result, the arguments have obvious politico-philosophic overtones. Though this aspect of the discussions will be avoided here, it is important to notice that, at least on the crowding out issue, there is a high correlation between most economists' political prejudices and their attitude to this question.

Within the Keynesian paradigm an increase in government expenditure would increase the level of national income by some multiple of the initial expenditure, through the multiplier process. Some resources would thus be acquired by the public sector, but the resulting income of the private sector would be even greater than it was before. This picture may be correct for the situation of a deep depression, but it would not seem to characterise the behaviour of modern economies closer to the full employment level of output. Crowding out can be said to occur when an increase in government expenditure of, say, £100m leads to an increase in national income of less than £100m. In other words, crowding out is associated

142

with the existence of a multiplier effect of less than unity. This is so called because it means that, as a result of resources being diverted into the public sector, the private sector is left with fewer resources than it had before. Super-crowding out arises when the multiplier is negative. Even if the multiplier is greater than unity there may be 'partial' crowding out in some areas. For example, investment may fall even if consumption has risen by a greater amount.

It is important to realise that this attitude to state intervention is not new. Rather it is as old as economics itself. The Keynesian view is the misfit, though this does not make it wrong. Spencer and Yohe (1970), for example, point out that even Adam Smith believed that government spending financed by borrowing involved '. . . the destruction of some capital which had before existed in the country, by the perversion of some portion of the annual produce which had before been destined for the maintenance of productive labour, towards that of unproductive labour ' (*Wealth of Nations*, 1937 edn, p.878). Spencer and Yohe (p.15) also refer to Hawtrey's evidence to the Macmillan Committee in 1930: 'Hawtrey stated that whether the spending came out of taxes or loans from savings, the increased governmental expenditures would merely replace private expenditures.'

The recent resurgence of a belief in crowding out is clearly associated with the monetarist critique, but it did not flow directly from the work of Friedman himself.[1] Rather, the main impetus came from the work of Anderson and Jordan (1968). What they did was to run a reduced form regression of national income on current and lagged values of government expenditure and current and lagged values of the money stock. The results indicated that while the impact effect of expenditure was positive this was soon offset by negative effects, so that, '. . . A change in Federal spending financed by either borrowing or taxes has only a negligible effect on GNP over a period of about a year' (Carlson and Spencer 1975, p. 3). Monetary expansion, on the other hand, had a positive cumulative effect.

It is fair to record that the Anderson and Jordan result has been widely discredited. This is partly due to the failure of their equation on more recent data. But more important is the theoretical argument of Goldfeld and Blinder (1972) who point to the inaccuracy of reduced-form techniques when the government reacts systematically to the state of the economy. An intuitive explanation of the Goldfeld—Blinder point is presented by Chrystal and Alt (1979). Basically, if fiscal stabilisation policy is designed to offset the effects of fluctuations in an exogenous variable, there need be no correlation between income and the budget deficit even if fiscal policy is working *perfectly* as a stabiliser.

By now, of course, the intellectual bandwagon of crowding out is rolling so fast that it matters not whether what started it is correct. What is important for present purposes, however, is to understand how crowding out could occur in the context of the macro-models that have been used above. The reader can then form his own view about their relevance to reality.

A further important point to be aware of before proceeding is that the crowding out issue is often regarded as being identical to the question of the effects of the government budget restriction. The latter arises because if the government runs a budget deficit this must be financed either by money printing, borrowing or raising taxes. This restriction has often been ignored in the past, as indeed it is in all three textbook models above, as well as in the forecasting model. We shall see below that crowding out could occur even without a government budget equation but that, once the government's financing requirement is taken into account, crowding out becomes so much more likely as to be highly probable, except when there is considerable slack in the economy.

The IS—LM Classical Case

It was seen in Chapter 5 that one common interpretation of both the monetarist and the classical case arises if the demand for money is strictly proportional to income. The effect of this in terms of Model II is that the LM curve becomes vertical. This is illustrated in figure 9.1 where LM_c is the relevant curve. A shift of the IS curve from IS_1 to IS_2 caused by an increase in government expenditure in Model I (The Keynesian expenditure system) would have caused an increase in income

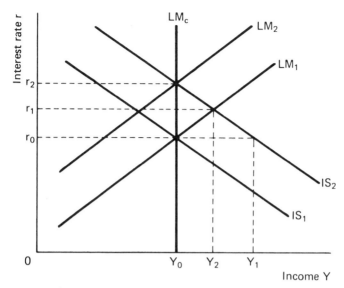

Figure 9.1

from Y_0 to Y_1. But with a vertical LM curve there can be no increase in income. Rather, the interest rate rises to r_2 until there has been a reduction in private investment equal to the initial rise in government expenditure. Even if the LM curve were upward sloping, as it clearly is in reality, there would still be *some* partial crowding out of private investment say on LM_1 at an interest rate of r_1. But the rise in income from Y_0 to Y_2 *could* represent a multiplier in excess of unity.

Other Model II Possibilities

A number of other cases are listed by Carlson and Spencer (1975) and it is convenient to present these among others, though some of them would seem a bit unlikely.

1. The Expectations Effect

At one point in the 'General Theory' Keynes himself suggested that a government expenditure programme could, in 'the confused psychology which often prevails', have an adverse effect on confidence. This could cause either an offsetting reduction in private investment or an upward shift in the LM curve. Both could cause crowding out with respect to income and the latter would involve a higher interest rate. This case seems unlikely to be of general importance, though it may apply in certain unusual circumstances.

2. Horizontal IS Curve

If investment were perfectly elastic with respect to the interest rate, the IS curve would be horizontal and fiscal policy would not shift it. Since national income is fixed by the LM curve, a rise in government expenditure would be exactly offset by a reduction in private expenditures. This is a pathological case which can be immediately dismissed as unreasonable.

3. Direct Substitution Effects

There may be some areas in which government expenditures provide services which the private sector would otherwise buy for themselves. Thus it is possible that there is some direct substitutability between state and private expenditures, but it is not very likely that this substitutability is of major significance at the margin.

4. Full Employment Price Level Effect

It should go without saying that if the initial position of the economy is at full employment, say at $r_0 Y_0$ in figure 9.1, there can be no increase in income. A shift in the IS curve to IS_2 will lead to a price level rise which will shift the LM curve to LM_2. Government expenditure will necessarily have a multiplier effect of zero, and again it will lead to an equal reduction in private investment.

5. Financing Effect — The Budget Restriction

The case which has been emphasised by Friedman relies upon the fact that sales of debt by the government will reinforce the negative feedback already noted in Model II. Consider the initial position in figure 9.1 at $r_0 Y_0$ on IS_1 and LM_1. An increase in government expenditure shifts the IS curve to IS_2 and the economy to $r_1 Y_2$. This rise in the interest rate is due to the increased transactions demand for money coupled with a fixed money supply. The rise in the budget deficit will have to be financed by sales of government debt which will put further upward pressure on interest rates. This upward pressure will be cumulative, so long as the deficit persists, whereas the initial multiplier is of a once-and-for-all nature. Thus any positive initial effect on income will eventually be offset by the negative cumulative effect of debt sales on private investment expenditures.

6. Balanced Budget Multiplier

Even in Model I, if an increase in government expenditure is financed by raising income taxes, the so-called balanced budget multiplier would be equal to unity. In Model II, however, since there is some rise in income with a fixed money supply, interest rates will have to rise. There will be some reduction in private investment and so the balanced budget multiplier becomes less than unity. Thus an increase in government expenditure financed by raising taxes will almost certainly involve some crowding out.

Crowding Out in Model III

It should be clear that, apart from case 4 above where output is fixed, if we add a supply side to the model, crowding out will be even more likely to occur. Consider, for example, the version of Model III outlined in Chapter 8. This is pictured in figure 9.2. The short-run aggregate supply curve AS_s is upward sloping because labour supply depends upon expected prices, whereas demand for labour depends upon actual prices. There is a rise in output in the short run because expectations lag behind actuality and so there is a temporary fall in the real wage. More labour is employed and more output produced.

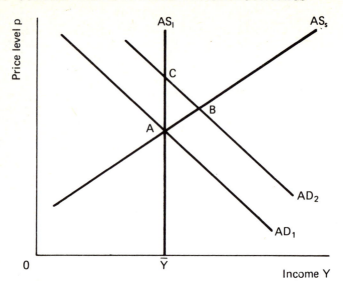

Figure 9.2

An initial increase in government expenditure would move the economy from A to B (ignoring the government budget constraint). However, over time price expectations will catch up with reality and, as they do, the short-run aggregate supply curve will shift up to the left. Eventually the economy will settle again at C where output is on the long-run aggregate supply curve. All the increase in government expenditure will have crowded out private expenditures of an equal amount. Largely it will be private investment crowded out since the fall in the real money stock will raise interest rates. Thus the story we are left with from this model is that crowding out is quite likely in the long run but there may be a short period during which government expenditure leads to income increases through the multiplier process. Only if the economy could be shown to start off well to the left of the AS$_l$ curve, and not to be there because of an inflation cycle, could we argue that there was a chance that there would be no long-run crowding out.

An additional factor which could increase the likelihood of *short-run* crowding out would be if price expectations are formed 'rationally', in the sense defined in Chapter 5.

Above it has implicitly been assumed that price expectations are formed as a revision from the prediction error made last time. If, however, all actors understand the model and realise that the expansion of government expenditure is going to raise prices, it could be that there will be no short-run output gain at all. Rather, the AS_s curve will shift up rapidly and the economy will go straight from A to C. This is the source of the argument that only unanticipated policy changes will have any real effects.

The remaining question concerns the position of the long-run supply curve. It has been argued that this will be positioned at the 'natural' level of output. This is basically determined from year to year by the underlying growth trend of the economy. It would seem from the above analysis that the only chance of long-run crowding out *not* occurring is if rises in government expenditure can somehow increase the underlying growth potential of the economy. This is certainly possible in principle but the most vociferous commentators on this issue believe that exactly the opposite will occur. Brunner and Meltzer (1976, p. 769), for example, argue that:

> Reduction in the output of the private sector could, in principle, be offset by the increased output of the public sector . . . It does not happen. Instead, there are loans or subsidies to enterprises that earn no profit or suffer large losses. Private saving is directed, in this case, toward enterprises that often do not earn rates of return equal to the interest on the bonds issued to finance the government budget deficit. Or, investment is used to increase 'prestige' as in the case of Concorde, national airlines, steamship lines and other enterprises that operate at negative rates of return. These enterprises direct material, skilled labour, and capital toward less productive uses than the private output that is crowded out. The list of such enterprises can be expanded by every knowledgeable reader.
>
> Absorption of labour by the government does not substitute public output for private output of equivalent value. Much public employment has the opposite effect. Complex rules and regulations absorb the time of civil servants and create demands in the private sector for lawyers, accountants, negotiators and clerks to keep abreast of the rules, to fill out the forms and hopefully to obtain more favourable interpretations than competitors have obtained.
>
> Employment is generated by this process, but much of the output produced by the employees has little value to society. More

efficient output is crowded out, replaced by records, completed forms and administrative decrees that in the aggregate subtract more than they add to wealth and to welfare.

We shall return to this question a little later in the chapter.

Crowding out in the Treasury Model

It is fortunate that Lewis and Ormerod (1979) have published the results of simulations on the Treasury and National Institute models as they existed in March 1978. We shall concentrate on the Treasury model as this is the one outlined in Chapter 2. For the purposes of this exercise, however, 'a small set of provisional monetary relationships' was added to the model. This should be kept in mind although, for the simulations reported here, interest rates were held fixed so this kind of monetary feedback is not included.

Multiplier Effect on Real GDP of Various Policies in the Treasury Model

Table 9.1 reports the multiplier effects produced in the Treasury model as a result of a number of different initial changes. The first simulation is for a rise of government consumption of £100m, holding interest rates, exchange rate and earnings fixed. This is the nearest thing possible in the model to the idea of the Keynesian multiplier. What is most surprising is that even without interest rate or price level feedbacks and with no supply side and no budget constraint in the model, the multiplier turns out to be only unity. Allowance for any of these omitted factors would obviously introduce some crowding out. The second simulation proves this because, for the same experiment but with earnings and the exchange rate endogenised, the eventual multiplier rate is lowered to 0.8.

The difference in effect achieved by lowering income tax rather than raising expenditure is shown in simulation 3. Here it takes six years to build up to the full multiplier effect of 1.4, whereas the first simulation reached the ultimate value of 1

Table 9.1 Multipliers in Treasury Model

	Approximate multiplier after number of years					
	1	2	3	4	5	6
1. Government consumption + £100m, interest rate, earnings, exchange rate fixed.	1.1	1.05	1.0	1.0	1.0	1.0
2. Government consumption + £100m, interest rate fixed; earnings endogenous, floating exchange rate.	1.1	1.04	0.9	0.8	0.8	0.8
3. Income tax reduced £100m, interest rates fixed, earnings endogenous, floating exchange rate.	0.4	0.55	0.9	1.15	1.38	1.4
4. Balanced budget: increase of taxes and government expenditure of £100m; interest rate fixed, earnings endogenous, exchange rate floating	0.75	0.4	0	−0.4	−0.58	−0.6

within a couple of years. Finally, simulation 4 shows the effect of a balanced budget multiplier which is 0.75 in year 1, but falls to zero in year 3 and is −0.6 by year 6.

It is clear that the Treasury model, even as it stands, does have properties consistent with the existence of crowding out. Incorporation of other possible effects would be likely to reinforce these characteristics. This does not prove that the economy works this way, of course, but it does indicate that the question of crowding out must be taken seriously.

New Oxford or Old Glasgow: Bacon and Eltis

A particular version of the crowding out thesis that has had a great deal of attention in the UK, through the publication of a series of articles in the *Sunday Times,* is due to Bacon and Eltis (1976). Their basic point would seem to be the same as that made by Adam Smith exactly two centuries earlier, which is that, by the expansion of the public sector, there has been a 'perversion of some portion of the annual produce which had before been destined for the maintenance of productive labour, towards that of unproductive labour.'

Bacon and Eltis pursue their argument by dividing the economy into two sectors rather like the Scandinavian model. However, here the two sectors are defined by whether or not they produce a 'marketed' output. 'The economy's market sector must produce all exports . . . all investment and all the goods and services that workers buy. It is to be noted that the market sector will include the nationalised indutries in so far as these cover their costs through sales of output, as well as the private sectors of modern economies. It will exclude public services which are provided free of charge.' (p. 123)

Like many other groups in the UK, Bacon and Eltis base their analysis upon an identity (relying, no doubt, on the security of Kaldor's laws of arithmetic!). This is:

9.1 $\qquad i_m + b_m \equiv e_m - c_u - i_u$

> The proportion of marketed output that can be reinvested in the market sector (i_m) plus the proportion of marketed output that can be exported net (b_m) is definitionally equal to the rate of surplus of marketed output in the market sector (e_m) less the proportions of marketed output that are used up in consumption (c_u) and investment (i_u) outside the market sector.

Only marketed goods can go into exports, investment and towards satisfying personal consumption expenditure. The 'surplus' of the marketed sector is equal to its total output less what is consumed by the workers in the market sector themselves. This surplus of goods can either be reinvested in the market sector, exported or used up in the non-market sector in the form of consumption and investment. The basic Bacon and Eltis thesis is that Britain's growth and balance of payments problems can be substantially explained by the fact that non-market sector absorption of market sector surplus has crowded out market sector investment and exports.

It is a small step now to identify the non-market sector with the non-industrial public sector, including all those supported by social services such as old age pensioners. In these terms the argument is that expenditure and especially employment in the public sector is too great for the 'health' of the economy. This diagnosis is supported by a casual glance at productivity trends which show that productivity rises in the market sector whereas it is static in the public sector. Diversion of resources into the public sector thus reduces the average productivity growth for the economy as a whole. This is a dangerous argument, however, because public sector output is typically *measured* by its labour input. So there is no way productivity in the public sector can rise — by definition.

The Bacon and Eltis taxonomy undoubtedly provides an interesting framework within which to view the economy. However, their methodology at best establishes correlations but not causation. They do not establish that growth in the marketed sector, *which would otherwise have happened*, was prevented by the employment of resources, especially labour, in the public sector. The upward trend in unemployment over the last two decades would testify to that. Indeed, the argument could just as easily be reversed. Because of the slow output growth in the industrial sector coupled with a continued productivity growth, there has been a decline in the demand for labour in industry. As a result it is essential to expand other forms of employment.

One of the statistics used by Bacon and Eltis to support their thesis is the ratio of non-industrial to industrial employment. This ratio rose in the UK from 0.97 in 1961 to 1.3 in 1974, a percentage increase of 34% which was more than double the percentage rise in any comparable country. However, even after this big rise, it is worth noting that this ratio in the UK is still considerably smaller than in the USA and about the same as in Japan and France.

Even more worrying for Bacon and Eltis, however, is the breakdown of the categories of public sector employment.

The biggest growth in employment between 1961 and 1974 seems to be in medical services and education. It is hard to believe that nurses and schoolteachers could just as easily have been employed as car workers. However, it is abundantly clear that in most other economies, health services and education are *marketed* products. It is quite possible that, if these services had been sold and priced through the market, employment in them would have grown even faster though the significance of such an expansion would be far from clear.

The important point to notice here is that many of the services provided by the public sector such as health, education, police and leisure services could well be luxury goods. In other words, demand for them would rise more than in proportion to real income growth. There can be no presumption about the 'correct' size of the public sector without some analysis of the underlying demand for the goods involved. Even if these publicly produced goods were to be a constant proportion of total national output, the underlying production functions would lead to a *growing* proportion of all employment being in the public sector. Public sector services, being labour intensive, require a bigger growth of labour input for any given growth of output than do manufacturing industries.

While it would not be surprising to find a growth of government consumption more than in proportion to the growth in national income, particularly when health services and education are provided by the state, it is not at all clear that this has happened to any significant degree in the UK. Chrystal and Alt (1979), for example, find that the elasticity of government consumption with respect to GDP is not significantly different from unity over the period 1955–74. They also find that British experience is not at all out of line with other countries:

> Britain was a relatively big spender in 1955, with 17 per cent of GDP going to government consumption; in 1974, the figure was 20.5 per cent, smaller than in Denmark, Sweden and the US and similar to that of Germany. Moreover, the growth of the government share in GDP was comparatively slow in Britain over these two decades, outstripping only the expenditure growth in Italy, the Netherlands, France and the US... these modest results do suggest that the

British experience is not unique and that there are clearly no grounds for assuming that government expenditure in Britain has grown atypically fast, or takes an atypically large share of national income. The apparent growth in government consumption as a share of GDP since 1974 is in large part due to the decline in GDP relative to trend, rather than to any untoward rise in government consumption relative to its own trend. The rise in transfers from public to private sectors is largely due to the rise in unemployment. Both these trends would normally be accepted as 'automatic stabilisers', which are of general benefit to the economy.

Summary

The conclusion reached in this chapter is that, while crowding out must realistically be accepted as a property of reasonable macroeconomic models, it is far from an established truth that over-expansion of government expenditure has *actually* been responsible for any significant crowding out of the private sector in the UK in the last 25 years. Controversy in this area will, no doubt, continue indefinitely.

Note

1 Apart from any influence *Capitalism and Freedom* may have had.

10

Fine Tuning

Taxes milks, but, neighbor, you'll allow
Thet havin' things onsettled kills the cow.
LOWELL

The issue of the previous chapter was the *level* of state activity
in the economy. In this chapter we discuss the even more
vexed question of the *variability* of state activity. Is the
government itself a major source of instability in the economy
or is it a beneficent agency minimising the fluctuations in
the level of activity which arise from both external and internal
shocks? This issue is now the one which is of greatest controversy in the United States for, as Gordon (1978, p. 335)
observes, 'The great irony of the debate between the monetarists and non-monetarists is that the effect of money
on unemployment and inflation is not the central issue.' This
point was emphasised by Modigliani (1977), one of the
leading non-monetarists, in his presidential address to the
American Economic Association:

> ... 'We are all monetarists' — if by monetarism is meant assigning
> to the stock of money a major role in determining output and prices.
> Indeed, the list of those who have long been monetarists in this sense
> is quite extensive, including among others John Maynard Keynes as
> well as myself. . .
> In reality the distinguishing feature of the monetarist school and
> the real issue of disagreement with non-monetarists is not monetarism,
> but rather the role that should probably be assigned to stabilisation
> policies. Non-monetarists accept what I regard to be the fundamental
> practical message of The General Theory: that a private enterprise

economy using an intangible money *needs* to be stabilised, *can* be stabilised and therefore *should* be stabilised by appropriate monetary and fiscal policies. Monetarists by contrast take the view that there is no serious need to stabilise the economy; that even if there were a need, it could not be done, for stabilisation policies would be more likely to increase than to decrease instability, and, at least some monetarists would, I believe, go so far as to hold that, even in the unlikely event that stabilisation policies could on balance prove beneficial, the government should not be trusted with the necessary power.

It would be difficult in a UK context, while New Cambridge and hard-line Keynesians are still in business, to argue, as Modigliani does for the US, that 'there are in reality no serious analytical disagreements between leading monetarists and leading non-monetarists.' What this statement must be interpreted as meaning is that, at least in the US, it would be relatively easy to get agreement about the structure of the appropriate *static* model of the economy. What is at issue now is, rather, the *dynamic* properties of this model and the most common source of disturbances.

The monetarist position in the US, as summarised by Gordon (1978, p. 339), consists of four propositions:

1. Private spending patterns would be basically stable if it were not for erratic changes in government policy.
2. Any instability in private spending will be offset by flexible prices.
3. Attempts to counter any remaining instability through monetary and fiscal policy will do more harm than good.
4. Even if prices are not completely flexible in the short run, so that the level of unemployment may deviate from the natural rate, there can be no argument that prices become more flexible the longer the adjustment period allowed.

The non-monetarist counter to each of these propositions is as follows:

1. While the permanent income hypothesis does imply a certain stability in normal consumption, the same does not apply to durable consumption expenditure and business investment. Fluctuations in these due to changes

in attitudes and expectations should be offset by monetary and fiscal policy. In the UK context we would also
have to add that there may also be fluctuations originat-
ing overseas, as the two major depressions this century
have been associated with a contraction in world trade.
2. Prices are relatively inflexible downward. There was no
obvious tendency during the Great Depression for price
flexibility to eliminate unemployment.
3. Although there are obvious examples of periods when
monetary and fiscal policy have been abused (viz. Mr
Barber's policies of 1971–2), lessons have been learned
from these episodes and so policy is much more likely
to be stabilising in future. Indeed, in Britain policy was,
largely, stabilising in the 1950s and 1960s. The problem
in the early 1970s was that we did not understand the
significance of flexible exchange rates.
4. The period of time required for price flexibility to
restore the economy to the natural rate of unemployment is too long, particularly in terms of the time
horizon of politicians. For this reason they are bound to
try combinations of incomes policies and aggregate
demand policy to achieve their goals more quickly.

The critical difference between the two views is that one
group believes that the economy is basically stable and that
its adjustment properties cannot be improved upon by fallible
governments. The other group believes either that the
economy is basically unstable or that, if stable, it is so slow
to adjust that stabilisation policies are necessary and have a
realistic chance of improving the situation.

The two groups in the UK that have been most critical of
short-term stabilisation policy are New Cambridge and the
Monetarists. Their unity on this issue is, however, more
apparent than real. They are both critical for almost dia-
metrically opposite reasons. It will be argued below that New
Cambridge are in the wilderness on this issue and should be
allowed to remain there. The Monetarists, on the other hand,
were basically correct in pointing to the dangers of excess
fluctuations in the money stock but have gone too far in
suggesting a 'rule' to govern the money stock.

New Cambridge

The best known statement of the New Cambridge attack on stabilisation policy is to be found in their evidence to the Public Expenditure Committee (1974):

Given that decisions about public expenditure have been taken, and given that Government is prepared to specify its targets with respect to the balance of trade and employment, an appropriate ('par') rate of tax may be inferred which should not normally be changed for stabilisation reasons. The proposition that private expenditure as a whole is dependent on private income as a whole necessarily implies that no component of private expenditure exerts an independent ('exogenous') net influence on the level of output or fluctuations in it. To put the same thing another way, *it is implied that the only potentially destabilising agents are the Government's own actions* with regard to expenditure, taxation and credit on the one hand, and, on the other, foreign influences, particularly export demand and world commodity prices. Therefore, if the tax rate is changed from 'par' one or other of the two major policy objectives must be foregone.

It appears to have been the case that during the past twenty years or so, purely by chance, the fluctuations of UK exports, to the extent that these were induced by changes in world trade, have been roughly offset by changes in import prices attributable to the same cause. To the extent that this is true, fluctuations in world trade have generated very little disturbance either to the UK balance of payments or to real output in total, and the observed fluctuations in output have, to this extent, been *entirely* the consequence of the stabilisation measures.' (p. 5)

The implications of this argument are self evident. Because the private sector is basically stable, fluctuations must originate from the government or overseas. When the above was written (1974), external factors did not appear to have had any major destabilising effects, so the main destabilising agent must have been the government itself. The CEPG recommendation was then that, for a given level of government expenditure, tax rates should be set at that level which would yield the appropriate budget deficit at full employment to match the target level of the balance of payments.

What is peculiar to New Cambridge is the reason for the private sector stability. It is because private sector expenditures adjust to private sector incomes very quickly, so the sector as a whole returns to balance very rapidly as a result of any external disturbance. It is not at all clear why this observation precludes the origin of a disturbance being within the private sector, particularly if we interpret this 'balance' as an identity as above. Surely the private sector as a whole could be balanced even though the level of income at which it was balanced was fluctuating. In more conventional terms, the fact that saving equals investment is an equilibrium condition, and does not preclude fluctuations in investment (or saving, see Goodwin, 1972) from *causing* fluctuations in income.

The more conventional criticism of stabilisation policy is based upon the opposite view of the private sector. This is that private sector expenditures are extremely sticky and are very slow to adjust to changes in income and asset positions. The overwhelming weight of empirical research in economics since the war in many countries would seem to support this latter view. One dubious regression equation from the CEPG is not going to turn the tide on this issue in a hurry. Economic opinions are, after all, even more sticky than expenditure patterns.

Monetarists

A clear statement of the views of a British Monetarist is also available in the evidence to the Public Expenditure Committee (1974). The following is an extract from Laidler's submission:

> If one thinks only in terms of the direct connection between fiscal policy and aggregate demand the design of stabilisation policy looks reasonably straightforward. Set a target for income and employment, forecast private sector activity and the balance of payments on various assumptions about the scale of government activities and then pick the level of government activities that will achieve the desired targets ... this whole way of thinking about stabilisation policy is misconceived. I have argued that monetary policy and hence the indirect effects of fiscal policy that operate through monetary variables are of much greater importance than is usually accorded them. However, I have also argued that these effects are subject to long and difficult-to-predict lags and that they involve a complex dynamic interaction of income, employment, inflation and the balance of payments, the processes involved in which are only crudely understood.
>
> If this is the case the time horizon over which policies towards

macroeconomic stability are carried out should be much longer than it is at present; five or ten years rather than twelve to eighteen months. Such policies should rely heavily on controlling the rate of monetary expansion and they should also be based on a clear recognition that it is impossible in the current state of knowledge to 'fine tune' the economy on a year to year basis.

The substantive point of Laidler's remarks, that monetary factors should not be neglected, is surely correct and has now clearly been acknowledged in official circles. After all, in 1979, we are still living with the disastrous effects of the monetary expansion of 1971—3. It should also, probably, be admitted that there is no point in trying to use monetary policy to fine tune the economy on a year-to-year, let alone a quarter-to-quarter, basis. The effects of monetary policy, almost certainly, do have a long and varied lag. Whatever is done with the money stock, therefore, should be done slowly and with great moderation. However, it has not been established that the *best* thing to do is to establish a rule for money supply growth which cannot be deviated from for discretionary reasons in any circumstances. It would seem quite reasonable to suggest that monetary policy should 'lean gently against the wind' while going through no major lurches and certainly never be used again in an attempt to initiate a 'dash for growth.'

Laidler's main attack upon fiscal policy is not that it does not work but rather that it has monetary effects which should not be ignored. So long as the government budget constraint is incorporated into the policy analysis in an appropriate way, there is some degree of freedom for short-term stabilising fiscal policy so long as it does not blow the appropriate money supply target off course. It is inconceivable in the UK that a 'balanced budget' is likely to be adopted as the fiscal target, but the immediate question seems to be the correct division of fiscal stabilisation between automatic and discretionary effects. New Cambridge would argue that it should all be automatic. Discretionary changes which are quickly reversed are now recognised to do more harm than good. So it is likely that even major fiscal policy changes will be fewer and farther between than in the hectic days of 1973—5 when a pattern of two or three budgets a year seemed to be emerging.

It would, then, seem not unreasonable to accept Modigliani's conclusions as being valid for the UK as well as for the US

> . . . The monetarists have made a valid and most valuable contribution in establishing that our economy is far less unstable than the early Keynesians pictured it and in rehabilitating the role of money as a determinant of aggregate demand. They are wrong, however, in going as far as asserting that the economy is sufficiently shockproof that stabilisation policies are not needed. They have also made an important contribution in pointing out that such policies might in fact prove destabilising. This criticism has had a salutary effect on reassessing what stabilisation policies can and should do, and on trimming down fine-tuning ambitions. But their contention that post-war fluctuations resulted from an unstable money growth or that stabilisation policies decreased rather than increased stability just does not stand up to an impartial examination of the post-war record of the US and other industrial countries. Up to 1974, these policies have helped to keep the economy reasonably stable by historical standards, even though one can certainly point to some occasional failures. (Modigliani 1977, p. 17)

Rational Expectations

Brief mention was made in Chapter 5 of the idea of rational expectations (see also Sargent 1976 and Sargent and Wallace 1975). In short, this hypothesis says that agents will form expectations on the basis of the best available information in the context of the best available model. Mistakes will be made in expectations but these errors will be random. If they were not random, some systematic information would be being ignored, which is inconsistent with the theory. In terms of labour markets, the rational expectations hypothesis is sometimes taken to imply that there can only be random short-term deviations from the natural unemployment rate; however, this conclusion does not seem warranted if adjustment costs are part of the model.

There are two important implications normally drawn from this approach for stabilisation policy. The first is that any announced monetary and fiscal policies will be ineffective on the real economy because the effects will be entirely discounted. In terms of the aggregate demand and supply analysis of Chapter 8, any anticipated upward shift of the aggregate demand curve will be immediately matched by an upward shift in the short-run aggregate supply curve — leaving the economy at the same level of real output, i.e. on the long-run supply curve. The second implication is that any external shocks which can be anticipated will already be anticipated by the private sector. So there is no need for government stabilisation unless the government has superior information, which it does not by assumption. Indeed, unexpected changes in government behaviour become the major source of destabilisation.

The concept of rational expectations is interesting and important but it should be regarded as a polar case, rather like textbook perfect competition. It is an interesting conceptual experiment which is more appropriate to some circumstances than others. In the context of the macroeconomics of inflation and unemployment it seems hard to reconcile with the facts. For, as Modigliani again points out, '. . . If it were valid, deviations of unemployment from the natural rate would be small and transitory — in which case "The General Theory" would not have been written and neither would this paper' (Modigliani 1977, p. 6). However, the concept of rationality is quite robust and it will no doubt prove possible to incorporate it in models which exhibit sustained unemployment and, therefore, need stabilising. But at present the development of 'rational' models is in its infancy.

Optimal Control

A radically different approach to macroeconomic policy which is broadly in the Keynesian tradition has grown out of what is now known as 'The Theory of Economic Policy'. The basic idea of this is that stabilisation policy can be decided as the solution of a mathematical optimisation problem. This approach is associated particularly with the names of Tinbergen and Theil. The terminology, which is due to Tinbergen, has the government choosing values of the 'instrument' variables which it controls, in order to achieve desired values of 'target' variables which it would like to control, subject to the constraints imposed by the workings of the economy. More sophisticated formalisations have the target variables contributing to a government utility function. So the formal policy problem is to maximise utility subject to constraints by choosing appropriate instruments.

One major insight which comes from this approach is that the government needs at least as many independent instruments as there are targets in order to be able to achieve its goals. However, it is never quite clear with this approach whether it is meant to be normative or positive. If it were normative the aim of the exercise would be to tell the government what it *ought* to do in any particular situation. If it were positive the aim would be to explain why the government had behaved in any particular way. The latter would seem to have an important role to play as an analytical approach to understanding endogenous government behaviour (see Chrystal and Alt 1979), but there can be no doubt that the former has received more emphasis to date.

The branch of applied mathematics which is concerned with controlling dynamic systems is known as optimal control theory. Since economic systems are in reality also dynamic, it is natural that there should be attempts to apply this mathematics in this area. There are, however, two major obstacles to using this mathematics in a normative way as the principal method of deciding policy. The first is that it is exceedingly difficult to specify the objective function of policy makers. If this cannot be done, the problem cannot even potentially be solved. The second obstacle is that the analogue to the control of a physical system is not a very good one. One does not have to believe in completely rational expectations to see that the behaviour of the private sector would change if the control principles were ever known. Thus for optimal control theory to work, we need to know not only how the economy will work if the government does nothing, but also how it will work *whatever* the government does. Add to these the obvious problems of uncertainty, disagreement about the true model and the political constraints on economic policy and the normative applicability of control theory seems strictly limited.

There has recently been an official enquiry into the applicability of optimal control theory to economic policy in the

UK. This 'Committee on Policy Optimisation' (1978) was chaired by Professor R.J. Ball and hence known as the Ball Committee. The main issues are well covered in this report so we shall not dwell on them here. There is also a detailed description of the part played by economists, within the Treasury, in the making of economic policy. The main conclusion of the Ball Committee is that, while optimal control techniques should be encouraged in the context of model simulations designed to increase understanding of the forecasting models (and thus eventually the economy), it is unlikely that in the foreseeable future they will have a *direct* impact on the way in which economic policy is made.

Political Business Cycles

The final question that must be discussed is whether the political objectives of governments may influence the way economic policy is made. It is now becoming a firmly established part of the 'conventional wisdom' that political objectives do influence the pattern of stabilisation policy (see, for example, Brittan 1978, Frey 1978, and Frey and Schneider 1978). One form of political influence may be due to ideological differences between parties. For example, it is sometimes argued that the Labour Party gives a bigger weight to the unemployment target, whereas the Conservative Party gives a bigger weight to inflation. This may be true, but it is fair to record that it has yet to be demonstrated satisfactorily.

More widely accepted is the view that encumbent governments attempt to generate a boom immediately before elections in order to improve their chances of staying in office. The inflationary consequences of such booms are felt after the elections. So the political business cycle is characterised by unpopular deflation early in the life of a government followed by a sharp reflation and a boom as the election approaches. The problem with this popular view as Alt (1979) points out is that the evidence for it is not strong.

> If all there was to the problem was to see whether the first halves of parliamentary terms were times of stagnation and the second halves times of prosperity, there would be no empirical difficulty, as we

could simply count the numbers . . . Nordhaus (1975) did just this and came to negative conclusions. Studying parliamentary terms in nine Western countries (including the UK), he discovered clear electoral-cyclical boom-slump movements of the unemployment rate in three: Germany, the US and New Zealand. Similarly, Paldam (1977) investigated . . . cyclical movements in a large number of economic indicators and found little evidence of electoral-cyclical variation.

On the other hand, as Alt also records, 'real *per capita* personal disposable income is about one-third more likely to *accelerate* in an election year than in a non-election year.' But if this is all there is going for the theory, is it really enough? This could simply mean that governments choose the most favourable times to hold elections, which would not be very earth shattering. No doubt we should accept that some governments, sometimes, in some countries try to manipulate the economy for electoral advantage. However, the important question for economists is, do governments *systematically* cause cycles by conducting stabilisation policy in ways different from what would be recommended by any neutral economic adviser? If the answer were yes, the important question for political scientists would be, do they win elections as a result? The answer to the latter question, in the UK at least, would have to be an emphatic no. There are at least as many cases of encumbent parties losing elections which have been preceded by a boom in real incomes as there are of victories. Indeed, the only possible case in the UK since the war of a *political* pre-election boom followed by a victory and a post-election deflation was 1955.

The evidence concerning the influence of economic factors on political popularity is not at all clear cut. Any relationship there is seems to be extremely unstable, and it is far from demonstrable that real income is the only, or even the most important, factor. Thus it is far from proven that a real income boom will significantly improve re-election chances. Even more tricky, however, is the identification of an expansion in the economy as being generated for political purposes. For this we need to find not just that governments are stimulating the economy before elections but rather that they are doing so *in excess* of what neutral observers are recommending.

An alternative way of looking at the two questions posed above is to ask whether the electorate can be fooled in the short run and whether the government acts as if they can. Asking the question this way focuses attention on the electorate's expectations as well as upon the current state of affairs. If electors are fully 'rational' they will anticipate the post-election deflation and so there will be no benefit for the encumbent party in running a pre-election boom. Macrae (1977) incorporates expectations explicitly by distinguishing between a myopic and a strategic electorate. A myopic electorate only considers the current state of the economy, whereas strategic voters have a longer time horizon. Macrae's results for the US appear to show that the government assumed myopia from 1960–8 but strategic voting before and after. After applying Macrae's model to the UK Chrystal and Alt (1980) conclude that, 'the myopic hypothesis never significantly outperforms the strategic hypothesis'. And they are thus led to conclude that, ' . . . while on some occasions the government may indeed have manipulated unemployment with a vote loss or social welfare function in mind, there is no evidence that the desire to win the *next* election, as distinct from remaining in office as long as possible, was the motivation'.

Thus we must conclude that the evidence for a political business cycle in Britain is, if anything, negative. There can be no presumption that the government manipulates the economy on the assumption of a short-sighted electorate. Neither would it seem that the theory provides a very accurate predictor of the timing of elections. Brittan (1978) was, for example, not alone in confidently predicting, in late June, that the Prime Minister was 'going to the country in the autumn'. The basis for this prediction was a fast rate of growth of real disposable income during 1977–8. However, the autumn passed, the winter of 1978–9 turned into yet another post-incomes-policy period of industrial and public sector strife (similar to 1969 and 1974 and hence predictable) and yet the election materialised in May 1979.

What appears to be a more sophisticated attempt to incorporate political goals into economic policy analysis is provided by Frey and Schneider (1978). They develop what they call a 'politico-economic' model of the UK. There are two elements to this. First, government popularity depends upon certain economic variables. Second, various components of government expenditure are shown to be altered as a result of popularity, time to elections and the political make up of the encumbent party. In reality, however, the popularity function is unstable with respect to economic factors and is dominated by a trend and an inter-election cycle. Chrystal and Alt (1980) also show that if government expenditure and revenue are related to trend GDP, virtually all the political factors drop out. The only significant political factor to remain is that transfers are higher under Labour than Conservative Governments, as might be expected. We must, therefore, conclude that electoral-cyclical and politico-economic explanations of budgetary policy in the UK are not well founded.

Summary

A fairly strong case has been made for arguing that monetary and fiscal policy are such 'blunt instruments' that the possibilities for 'fine tuning' the economy are severely limited. The economy is slow to react and the lags involved make it difficult to have any major effects within the period of reasonably accurate forecasts. However, this does not mean that the government should abandon all attempts at stabilisation and simply balance the budget or set a rigid rule for money supply growth. At the very least, automatic stabilisers should be allowed to operate so that public sector demand for resources expands during a depression and contracts during a boom. The appropriate degree of 'discretionary' stabilisation is a matter of judgement and, of course, controversy.

There appears to be no well established case for the existence of an electoral economic cycle in the UK, though this does not prove that a different political system would not have produced better economic policies.

11

An Example:
Oil, Crisis to Crisis

Economy is too late at the bottom of the purse
SENECA

One of the most difficult problems that arises in trying to
discuss contrasting views about how the economy works is
that it is difficult to take ideas out of context, and yet
different commentators are rarely worried about the same
precise problem. As a result, the context of views is always
slightly different. The purpose of this chapter is to provide a
highly specific context, or to be more precise, two highly
specific contexts, in terms of which to contrast the major
analytical approaches to macroeconomics. The examples we
shall take are, first, the case of an exogenous price rise in a
major imported material, i.e. oil, and the second is that of an
indigenous discovery of a major supply of oil. The assignment
of various aspects of the argument to one school or another,
of course, involves a certain amount of licence.

The Oil Price Rise

The basic problem, then, is how do we analyse particular
events that arise and, as a result, what policy recommendations
would we make. The first problem chosen as an example is
that of a sudden substantial rise in the price of a major
import. This is obviously an important problem because it is

one that has recently been experienced and so we can try to see why policy reacted as it did. There is already one attempt, by Miller (1976), in the literature to analyse this problem in similar terms, and it is fair to record that the idea for this chapter derives in large part from that paper.

The principal way in which the policy makers in the UK looked at the problem seems to be through orthodox Keynesian eyes. In the context of Model I, imports are a leakage from the circular flow system so they affect the economy just like a massive increase in indirect taxes. The tax revenue, however, accrues to foreigners. A typical figure quoted for the size of this increased import bill was £1500m. A clear example of how a Keynesian should see this problem is provided by G.D.N. Worswick, the Director of the National Institute, in his evidence to the Public Expenditure Committee:

> If nothing is done about the substantial rise in the price of oil, that figure of £1500m will be taken out of the system. There will be that much less spent in the following period and there will be a contraction of demand and a contraction of output in due course together with a contraction of employment. In this case the rise in the price of oil has a profound contractionary effect on all countries. (p. 42)
>   ... When the government is making up its balance of the budget over the year as a whole it must allow for the fact that real consumption will be less than it would be if the price of oil had not risen ... The present Chancellor has said that he wishes to have a new look at the situation later in the year. As I see it now, he would need to be expansionary. (p. 43)

The effect of a rise in the value of imports can easily be analysed in the context of Model I. The initial position in figure 11.1 is with the aggregate expenditure line $C + I + G + X - P_0$. This gives an initial level of income equal to Y_0. An increase in the value of imports represents a greater 'leakage' of expenditure from the circular flow, so the aggregate expenditure line falls to $C + I + G + X - P_1$. This will lead, through the downward multiplier effect, to a lower level of income Y_1. We would normally expect this downward fall in income to be accompanied by an increase in unemployment. This is why the Keynesian response to the oil crisis was to point to the dangers of a depression and to propose a reflation. Offsetting policies on the part of the government would simply involve either increasing expenditure or reducing

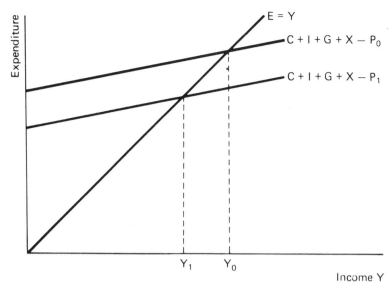

Figure 11.1

taxes so that aggregate expenditure shifts back towards its original position. The balance of payments deficit is thus reinforced.

The problem, of course, is not really as simple as that. For one thing we have said nothing at all about inflation. More importantly in the present context, however, the concept of income is ambiguous. The simplest way to see this is to ask what would have happened if the elasticity of demand for oil had been unity. The import bill would have remained constant following the oil price rise. But does this mean that domestic income would have been unchanged? The answer is clearly no. Although there is no direct change in real GDP because physical output and the GDP deflator are unchanged, since the value of the things we produce has fallen relative to the things we buy from abroad, domestic income has unambiguously fallen in a real and more general way. What this means is that, even if there were no impact effect on unemployment, the possibilities for domestic absorption have fallen. There has to be a fall in domestic real income.

While domestic income has to fall owing to this terms-of-trade loss, it does not necessarily follow that some reflation should not be applied. Miller argues that the view at the time was that the required fall in income was less than the fall from Y_0 to Y_1 in figure 11.1 and this is why expansionary measures were advocated. The problem with this approach, of course, is that even if it were successful in avoiding unemployment in the short run, it certainly increases inflation, which many would argue would increase unemployment even more in the long run. The outcome would appear to be consistent with this latter view. Unemployment did not rise as rapidly in the UK through 1974 and 1975 as it did in many other countries, whereas the inflationary experience was considerably worse in the UK. Unemployment in the UK, however, continued to rise subsequently, though in many countries it started to fall after 1976.

Miller concludes that while Keynesians were not unaware that there would be 'imported inflation', they believed that a gradual return to full employment should be possible through 'expansionary fiscal policy and permissive monetary policy'. In strict contrast to this Miller believes that ' . . . the Monetarist logic predicted no inflation or recession as a consequence of the change in the terms of trade so long as fiscal and monetary policy were unchanged'. Miller bases his analysis of the Monetarist position upon the summary of the evidence presented by Laidler to the Expenditure Committee. However, this summary was either written by the Committee members themselves or by the Civil Service. Laidler's own evidence does not bear the interpretation Miller puts upon it (nor, in reality, does the summary).

The first point to notice about Laidler's evidence is that he is absolutely clear that ' . . . If oil prices have gone up and the terms of trade have moved against this country, we are poorer, and it is impossible for people to protect their standards of living against that'. Secondly, he answers the question about the price level by reference to an earlier point about the net effect of a decrease in indirect taxes financed by higher direct taxes, at a given level of national income. There he says, 'If there were no net decrease in purchasing power, I cannot see how *ultimately* the price level would be different'. In contrast, the Director of the National Institute was reported to have argued, by analogy to an increase in indirect taxes; that inflation would rise because people would ask for and obtain higher wages to compensate for the higher oil price. Indirect taxes rising would be inflationary and more inflationary than income taxes of equal yield. To this Laidler replied: '. . . If it is the case that people notice that indirect taxes have changed the purchasing power of their gross incomes before they notice that direct ones have done so, I cannot believe that this is any more than a very *short-run* phenomenon. It is one thing, in any case, to ask for a wage increase and another thing to have it granted.'

The overwhelming impression that emerges from Laidler's evidence, in its entirety, can be expressed as two main points. First, the impact effects of the oil price rise should be clearly distinguished from the ultimate or long-run effects. Second, a clear distinction must be drawn between relative price changes and sustained inflation of the general price level. The oil price rise is a relative price change and, although it will undoubtedly raise the price index in the short run, it will only lead to a *long-run* rise in the price level if it is followed by monetary expansion. An appropriate framework for expounding the Monetarist analysis might be Model III.

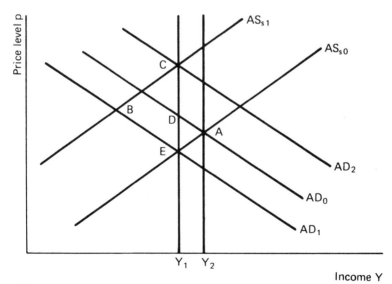

Figure 11.2

Consider the initial position at A in figure 11.2. The short-run aggregate supply curve can be thought of as depending on the expected price level, as outlined in Chapter 8. What then is the effect of a rise in the price of imports? First notice that, although the *physical* production possibilities of the economy are unchanged, since the relative price of domestic output has fallen, we should regard long-run aggregate supply as having fallen from Y_0 to Y_1 This is the terms-of-trade loss. There are two other effects. Firstly, there is a leftward shift of the short-run aggregate supply curve from AS_{S0} to AS_{S1}. This is due to the direct effect of import prices on the domestic price level plus any immediate effect on price expectations. The second effect is the Keynesian one. Aggregate *domestic* demand will move from AD_0 to AD_1 due to the rise in the import bill. Both Monetarists and Keynesians should accept the story so far. The impact effect is a move from A to a position like B. There has been a rise in the price level and an increase in unemployment associated with a decline in domestic output. The disagreement is about the next step in the argument.

The Keynesians do not have a next step. The economy has settled into a depression at B so expansionary fiscal policies are required. Raising aggregate demand will move the economy to C, thereby eliminating unemployment. The problem with this analysis, however, is that even C is not a full equilibrium. This is because AS_{S1} was drawn for an *expected* price level somewhere between that at A and that at B. As these price level expectations are revised upwards, the short-run AS curve will shift up further. If policy makers raise aggregate demand still further to avoid unemployment, this upward spiral will continue, as they found to their cost.

The Monetarist analysis points to the fact that B is not a point of full equilibrium. If the monetary and fiscal pressures which are due to the authorities remain unchanged, the economy will eventually return to a point somewhere in the region of D. This is because excess supply in some markets will cause some prices to fall, so eventually short-run AS will shift back down. Also there will be some northeastward shift of AD due to a change in the pattern of expenditures following the increase in import prices. The ultimate effect of the oil price rise on the import bill will, *ceteris paribus*, be less in the long run than in the short run because expenditure patterns take time to adjust. At D the price level may be slightly higher or lower than at A, but it will not be substantially different. The problem with this Monetarist analysis is that we have no information how long it will be before the economy returns from B to D. The problem with the Keynesian policy prescription is that it necessarily leads to a higher price level and, therefore, to faster inflation in the interim. At the time of writing, the UK is still suffering from that inflation. The key difference in analysis of the problem is that Monetarists see the economy as self-stabilising within a reasonable time period. Keynesians recommend policies to counter the impact effects alone. Keynes is dead, but someone will still be alive in the long run!

North Sea Oil

An almost opposite process is involved in the adjustment to the discovery of indigenous oil in the North Sea. This provides us with policy problems of a different kind. If the initial position were at E in figure 11.2, the discovery of oil would induce a once-and-for-all shift of the long-run supply curve, say, from Q_1 to Q_0. If nothing else happened there would be a decline in the equilibrium price level. However, there will certainly also be a rightward shift in AD due to this switch of expenditure from imports to domestic production. The multiplier effects on domestic expenditure could exceed the increase in output, thus requiring a policy deflation to avoid a rise in the price level.

The precise macroeconomic effects of North Sea oil are probably not known and it is not about these that there has been any serious discussion. Rather, the debate has centred upon the balance of payments effects and the appropriate policy *vis à vis* the exchange rate. There are two points of controversy which arise here. One concerns the long-term forecast of the balance of payments gain due to North Sea oil. The other concerns the correct exchange rate policy to adopt.

To make the two contrasting views of the balance of payments as clear as possible, let us assume that the economy has a static level of national income and starts off with a balance in the trade account. There is also a fixed exchange rate. A discovery of oil produces a step up in the level of income which is then constant again at the new higher level. What happens to the balance of payments?

Keynesians would argue that, since the new output is import saving, there will be a balance of payments gain roughly equal to the output of oil less interest on exploration capital borrowed abroad. The overall effect is actually calculated by shifting the aggregate expenditure function by the amount of the oil saving, but typical forecasts using Keynesian techniques have usually produced forecasts of this order. Within this framework the recommendation for policy that results is often to increase government expenditure or reduce taxes permanently as a way of spending the 'oil revenue'.

The monetary approach to the balance of payments would suggest a completely different analysis of this problem. The rise in income due to North Sea oil will increase demand for real money balances. If these balances are provided by domestic credit expansion *there will be no net balance of payments surplus at all.* Only if there is no (or little) domestic credit expansion will there be any balance of payments, surplus. Even then, however, the balance of payments surplus will be transitory, lasting only as long as is necessary to provide the required *once-and-for-all* rise in real balances. There will thus also be a once-and-for-all rise in reserves.

The reason for the argument that the effect is once-and-for-all is that the balance of payments is the difference between income and expenditure. Higher income leads to a higher desired stock of money (or indeed financial assets). While this stock is being built income will exceed expenditure. Once the desired stock is achieved, expenditure will equal income and the balance of payments will be zero. Thus the argument that the balance of payments surplus is transitory *does not* depend either upon exhaustion of oil wells or expansionary fiscal policy. Indeed, both of these would *inevitably* lead to further balance of payments deficits in the future.

In the mid-1970s the (Keynesian) forecasters were confidently predicting vast balance of payments surpluses for 1979 and the early 1980s on the basis of predicted oil production. Oil production does not seem to have been over-estimated, but the balance of payments gain clearly has. This does not necessarily invalidate the original forecasts since 'other things' have not remained constant. The monetary approach would, however, have led us to expect this outcome all along. The deficit is a thing of the past! . . . and the future?

Exchange Rate Protection

Even if the balance of payments gain is only temporary, should the authorities allow the exchange rate to appreciate or should they hold it down and increase their stock of international reserves?

Monetarists have been inclined to argue that the exchange rate should be allowed to appreciate. The real balances the economy requires will thereby be provided by upvaluing the existing stock (relative to what they would otherwise be). The benefit of doing this is that, during the transition, the domestic inflation rate would be lower than otherwise. This could, therefore, speed up the slow process of expurgating inflationary expectations from the system and make the cost of returning to a low and stable inflation rate that much less in terms of unemployment.

The more likely response of a British Keynesian to this question is to argue that appreciation of the currency is likely to harm the 'competitive position' of our exporters. Appreciation of the currency will either raise the foreign currency price of our exports or it will reduce the profitability of exporting. Accordingly, it is argued, there will be a decline in export industries and a layoff of labour in this sector. This is particularly serious in the light of the fact that North Sea oil will only last 10 or 15 years. We will then be reliant upon our export industries once more to earn us a living. The correct thing for the government to do, therefore, is to pre-serve the competitive position of our exporters by holding the exchange rate down and taking the 'profit' in the form of reserves.

The worrying thing about this argument is its plausibility. On the one hand, devaluation is bad because of the associated real income loss, yet on the other revaluation is bad because it harms exporters. It is also rather troublesome that the economies with the most successful export sectors, such as West Germany and Japan, have achieved this success despite the apparent handicap of appreciating currencies.

The real problem in analysing this issue, however, is that the framework of a macroeconomic model is not the appropriate vehicle of thought. Once we have an issue where effects differ between industry groups an explicit general equilibrium framework is required. Indeed, Corden (1978a, 1978b) has recently referred to exactly this question as being one of 'exchange rate protection.' Corden draws a distinction within tradeables between the 'booming' sector (in our case, North Sea oil) and the 'lagging' sector (other manufactured exportables). The issue is whether to hold down the exchange rate and thereby protect the lagging sector (and indeed the booming sector) relative to the non-tradeables sector.

It is beyond the scope of this book to pursue the trade theoretical aspects of this problem any further. The optimal policy is by no means clear cut, though in global terms exchange rate protection, as with orthodox tariffs, must involve a second-best solution (or worse). It is sufficient for present purposes to have communicated the analogue between exchange rate protection and tariff policy.

North Sea oil will undoubtedly make us all better off, but there is no guarantee that it will make us less crisis prone. Only a better understanding of our economic environment can do that!

Summary

The Keynesian response to the 1973 oil crisis was to reflate the economy. This produced less unemployment in the short run but more inflation and probably more unemployment in the long run. Monetarists would have recommended maintaining the level of domestic monetary demand approximately constant.

The discovery of North Sea oil in Keynesian terms should give us a balance of payments improvement for as long as the oil lasts, though a Monetarist would argue that any balance of payments improvement would at best be transitory, even if the oil flow were perpetual.

12

The Truth

The 1970s have taught us that macroeconomics is about aggregate supply, not just aggregate demand.
ROBERT GORDON

The truth is that we do not know precisely how the economy works, and to a considerable degree we shall never know. Nonetheless the macroeconomy continues to dominate our everyday lives whether through inflation or incomes policies or unemployment. There is no possibility that people will lose interest in trying to understand this environment as well as they can, and despite many apparent failures economists will be expected to have some expertise in this area.

The Evolution of Macroeconomics

The pattern of evolution of macroeconomics in the 1950s and early 1960s seemed to be quite clear. The core of the 'true' model was initially provided by the Keynesian income —expenditure system. Research was aimed at improving the explanatory power of the main expenditure functions — the consumption function, the investment function and the import and export functions. Major progress was made in the 1950s on the consumption function by the advent of the permanent income and life cycle hypotheses. Major progress seemed to be on the way in investment in the 1960s through the application of dynamic optimisation models of firms' behaviour .

The Monetarist critique of the income—expenditure model appeared easy to handle in the mid-1960s. The model widely regarded as being derived from the General Theory was, after all, the IS—LM model. This had a monetary sector. A monetary sector represented a net addition to the model and in no way detracted from the relevance of work done on the expenditure functions themselves. In the US the monetary sector was readily adopted and the only point of controversy seemed to be the values of certain elasticities — notably the interest elasticity of demand for money and the interest elasticity of investment. In Britain a group of hardliners centred on Cambridge have never accepted this natural evolution.

Even the IS—LM model was deficient in so far as it was unable to handle situations where both the price level and the level of real income were variable. In this case necessity was the mother of the Phillips curve. The framework of the Phillips curve at last seemed to offer the relationship which would 'close' the model. The analytical framework was complete. All that was required was for ever-increasing empirical work on the basic expenditure functions, the Phillips curve and the demand for money to home in on the true relationships with ever-increasing accuracy.

The development of forecasting models lagged behind the development of the textbook models — especially in the UK. Nonetheless, by 1968 there were several models of this type available in the US. A typical example is provided by the Wharton Model which was outlined in Evans (1969). This was basically a slightly disaggregated expenditure system, but interest rates and the price level were endogenous to the system. In the UK the Treasury did not have an operational computer-based forecasting system until as recently as 1970 though, as we have seen, it has made major progress since then. The early versions of the Treasury model were of course strictly in the income—expenditure tradition with all monetary variables (such as interest rates and the price level) being exogenous. In many ways, however, the forecasters in the UK — especially within the Treasury and the London Business School — are now leading the way in macroeconomics despite starting from behind. Recent developments in the estimation of consumption functions have been stimulated and contributed to by Treasury forecasters. And a lead has been given by the Treasury in developing a model of the monetary sector as well as of capital flows. The London Business School forecasters have taken the lead in analysing the international transmission of inflation. It could well be argued that students should now look to forecasting models, rather then textbooks, if they wish to keep up to date with macroeconomics in Britain.

The Crisis in Macroeconomics

The evolutionary process of the macroeconomic model, of course, did not home in upon the 'true' version of the IS–LM model. Life was good for the macroeconomist in 1966. It was not so easy in 1976. By the latter date, just about every empirical macroeconomic relationship, which had formerly fitted well, had broken down. Keynesians pointed to the demand for money functions, but failure was equally apparent in the expenditure functions and the Phillips curve. Even the beloved consumption function had provided a massive over-prediction of consumption expenditure in 1974 and 1975. Was macroeconomics on the wrong lines or was there a simpler explanation?

The answer that seems appropriate on the basis of the analysis of this book is that macroeconomics was not entirely on the wrong lines. The problem was that the range of experience that early models were tested against was very limited. Macroeconomic models did not exist before the Second World War. The economic environment of the 1950s and early 1960s was extremely unusual as a historical episode. First, there was almost global fixity of exchange rates. Second, world prices – especially commodity prices – were almost completely static. And third, a single strong economy (the USA) had a dominant role in the world. It was the cornerstone of the exchange rate system and was the 'banker' country to the world. Yet, initially it did not abuse this position. Its policy-makers pursued 'conservative' macroeconomic policies until at least 1963. Up to this time, also, there was a general 'dollar shortage', so there was no question of the exchange value of the dollar coming under pressure. As we know only too well, the 'swinging sixties' changed all this. The first crack to appear in the UK was the devaluation of November 1967. This was the first change in the par value of sterling for nearly 20 years. A devaluation must always be expected to change the domestic inflation rate. What seems surprising now is that anyone was surprised by the experience of simultaneously rising inflation and rising unemployment through 1969. The restrictive aggregate demand policies, which were agreed to be necessary after devaluation, were responsible for rising unemployment, while the devaluation itself caused rising prices. The wage explosion of 1969 was widely interpreted by Keynesians as proof of the role of exogenous trade union militancy as this occurred despite rising unemployment. However, a more sensible explantion would include a 'catch-up' of public sector wages following a 'pay pause' as well as the lagged adjustment of price expectations following the devaluation.

The deterioration in the inflationary experience within the UK took place against a background of slowly accelerating world inflation. The domestic 'War on Poverty' of the early Johnson years in the USA had been superseded by an external war of a different kind, in Vietnam. Both were financed to a large degree by deficit spending. The dollar shortage soon gave way to a dollar glut. General convertibility of dollars into gold was halted in March 1968. And the final nail in the coffin of the international monetary system, which had worked so well since the Second World War, came on 15 August 1971, when President Nixon 'closed the gold window' even to other central banks. In effect, the dollar was floated.

The effect upon the world economy was traumatic. The massive outflow of dollars from the US between 1969 and 1972 had the effect of doubling official international reserves over a period of about three years. At the same time it had become permissible for exchange rates to float. This meant that at the same time as reserves were generally rising, the apparent need for reserves was actually being reduced. It is no coincidence that policy-makers in most major economies adopted expansionary policies in these circumstances. The USA was already inflating. The commodity price boom of 1973 can be regarded as a 'leading indicator' of the world-wide inflation which inevitably followed.

The inflationary experience of the UK in the 1970s was even worse than the typical world experience. There can be little doubt that the reason for this is the excessively expansionary monetary and fiscal policies of 1971–2. This was Mr Barber's 'Dash for Growth'. It is easy with hindsight to notice that, if Mr Barber had maintained a neutral stance at this time, the UK economy would have been in a very much stronger position subsequently. Industrial production in 1977 was still lower than it had been in 1972.

There are two simple reasons why macroeconomic models broke down. The first is that a move from fixed to floating exchange rates involves a structural change in the monetary sector. With fixed exchange rates the scope for independent monetary policy is limited. The domestic money supply and domestic interest rates are directly affected by the balance of payments. With floating exchange rates all this changes. Domestic nominal money supply is no longer affected by the balance of payments and domestic nominal interest rates rise as domestic inflation rises. Structural change in the UK monetary system was compounded by the reforms of 'Competition and Credit Control.'

The second reason for the breakdown of macro-models was the inflation itself. Although there are many well documented examples of hyper-inflations in other countries – notably in Central Europe after the First World War and in Latin America more recently – the inflation of the 1970s is unprecedented in peacetime UK economic history. The inflation rate of 1975–6 was five or ten times worse than the average inflation rate experienced up to that time by the typical UK adult citizen.

Inflation seems to have had two related effects on macro-economic relationships. First it affects nominal variables directly. This means that actors behave in the light of the expected rate of inflation both in setting prices and wages and in choosing between real and nominal assets. With respect to the Phillips curve, this means that the old relationship was a special short-run case for a particular (low) expected inflation rate. Second, inflation seems to have changed the relationships between real variables. Even the consumption function, which relates real consumption to real income, has been found to shift as a result of inflation. There could be many reasons for this – restoring real liquid assets; precautionary saving; false signals, etc. – but it will probably be some time before the possibilities can be safely assessed.

The important point to notice, however, is that the early models did not fail because they were wrong all along. They failed because they were designed for a different set of circumstances. The automobile is not a failure because it cannot float on water. Both the income–expenditure model and the IS–LM model assume fixed prices. The assumption of fixed prices and variable outputs is useful in periods like the 1930s or even the 1950s. But it should be no surprise that more attention has recently been given to the opposite, i.e. flexible (upwards) prices and fixed outputs. The latter is associated with the idea of the 'natural' rate of output and the 'natural' level of unemployment. A period of rapidly rising prices and stagnant output will obviously lend support to this kind of view of the world.

The natural rate hypothesis, however, does not tell us a great deal about the short-run behaviour of the economy which has been the traditional concern of macroeconomics, but it does give us a clue as to where to look. The main difference between the Keynesian model in which prices are fixed and output is elastic and the 'rational' models in which long-run output is fixed and prices are elastic, is in the presumed supply side behaviour of both workers and firms. In the former there is always excess supply at ruling prices and wages. In the latter expectations anticipate fully so that *nominal* prices and wages adjust to expenditure changes, but real supplies do not change at all. The truth, in the short run, is obviously in between these two extremes. Thus it is the supply side of the economy which holds the missing key to explaining price and output dynamics in the short run. We must thus concur with Gordon's (1978, p. viii) assertion that: 'The 1970s have taught us that macroeconomics is about aggregate supply, not just aggregate demand.'

Sidelines

The economists who have now moved on to working on supply side dynamics, strangely, seem to be those who in the UK had earlier earned the label of 'Monetarist.' At the very least it should be abundantly clear that the range of concern of a 'Monetarist' extends rather further than the assertion that the price level is proportional to the money stock. Indeed it will probably be easier if the term 'Monetarist' is reserved for the latter point of view and positions *vis à vis* more current issues can be characterised by a new terminology.

The general disenchantment with 'standard' macroeconomics in the early 1970s gave fuel for splinter groups which set off at a tangent to the evolution of the mainstream. The Monetarist critique of Keynesian economics has undoubtedly led to a net increase in our understanding of the macroeconomy. Nothing that Keynesians got right has been abandoned, but much that they ignored has now been accounted for. Some groups in the UK, however, seem to be heading in completely the wrong direction. One such group is New Cambridge.

The New Cambridge approach to macroeconomics seems to be on a sideline heading backwards. There are three absolutely central areas in which New Cambridge are at variance with the main drift of the development of macroeconomics as it has been set out above. First, their approach to aggregate expenditures by which private sector expenditure adjusts to income extremely quickly, flies in the face of all that has been learnt in macroeconomics in the last 40 years. At best they would seem to be misguided; at worst, wrong. Second, the stubborn refusal to incorporate explicitly the behaviour of monetary variables severely limits from the start the applicability of their models. Even the Treasury has been quick to realise the importance of the monetary sector, especially when the exchange rate is endogenous. Third, when inflation is the single biggest problem of our day, it is just not good enough to assume that the whole driving force of the inflation process comes from an arbitrary 'real wage target' which is blindly adhered to in complete independence from the state of the economy. Such a theory cannot be consistent with rational optimising behaviour on the part of anyone; it cannot even be a sensible rule of thumb!

The Way Forward

The first phase of the evolution of macroeconomics was concentrated on examination of expenditure flows. The second phase incorporated a stylised treatment of the holding of financial assets. There can be little doubt that the third and current phase should be characterised as investigating the supply side of the economy. The Keynesian assumptions of perfectly elastic outputs and exogenous prices and the 'rational expectations' view of exogenous ('natural') levels of output and employment accompanied by perfectly elastic prices are polar cases. The truth obviously lies somewhere in between, but it is by no means clear, in the present state of knowledge, that the former is a better assumption than the latter.

It is to be hoped that this book will encourage more students in the UK to do research in this area. Macroeconomics is an interesting and challenging subject. The frontiers of the subject are on the front pages of the newspapers every day. The fact that we do not have all the answers does not mean that new answers cannot be found. The explanation of problems like inflation and unemployment must remain the province of the economist. We should not be prepared to yield to the oratory of archbishops or politicians who see these problems as the result of social, political or moral phenomena. Economists who subcribe to these latter views are doing us all a disservice.

Controversies

Controversies will no doubt continue. Indeed controversies must continue if progress is to be made. No professional journal has ever accepted a paper which says 'I agree with everything that has been said on this issue', — some disagreement is essential for survival. However, it is to be hoped that future controversies will not be conducted with the vitriolic dogmatism that has often characterised 'Cambridge contro-versies' (both in capital theory and macroeconomics) in the past. In any event we should have learnt at least one thing from our recent experience which is that, in the long run, both parties to any controversy will be thought to have been wrong.

References

Alt J., 'Political business cycles in Britain' in P. Whiteley (ed.), *Models of Political Economy*, Sage 1979.

Alt J. and Chrystal K.A., 'Endogenous government behaviour: overture to a study of government expenditure,' University of Essex, Department of Economics, *Discussion Paper No. 108*, 1977.

Anderson L.C. and Jordan J.L., 'Monetary and fiscal actions: a test of their relative importance in economic stabilization,' Federal Reserve Bank of St. Louis *Monthly Review*, Nov. 1968.

Artis M.J. and Lewis, M.K., 'The demand for money in the UK 1963–1973,' *Manchester School* 1976.

Aukrust O., 'Inflation in the open economy: a Norwegian model,' in Krause and Salant 1977.

Bacon R. and Eltis W., *Britain's Economic Problem: Too Few Producers*, Macmillan 1976.

Ball J. and Burns T., 'The inflationary mechanism in the UK economy,' *American Economic Review*, September 1976.

Barro R.J. and Grossman H., *Money, Employment and Inflation*, Cambridge University Press 1976.

Bean C., 'The determination of consumers' expenditure in the UK', HM Treasury Working Paper No. 4, June 1978.

Beutel M., 'Class in contemporary Britain,' in Green and Nore 1977.

Blinder A., 'What's 'new' and what's 'Keynesian' in the 'New Cambridge' Keynesianism?' in Brunner and Meltzer 1978.

Branson W. and Litvack H., *Macroeconomics*, Harper and Row 1976.

Brittan S., 'The election and the economy,' *Financial Times*, 26 June, 1978, p. 8.

Brittan S., 'The dubious case for import controls for all,' *Financial Times*, 29 March, 1979.

Brunner K. and Meltzer A.H., 'Government, the private sector and "crowding out",' *The Banker*, July 1976, pp. 765—9.

Brunner K. and Meltzer A.H. (eds), 'Public policies in open economies,' Carnegie—Rochester Conference No. 9, Supplement to the *Journal of Monetary Economics* 1978.

Carlson K.M. and Spencer R.W., 'Crowding out and its critics,' Federal Reserve Bank of St. Louis *Monthly Review*, December 1975.

Chow G.C., 'Usefulness of imperfect models for the formulation of stabilization policies,' *Annals of Economic and Social Measurement* 1977.

Chrystal K.A. and Alt J., 'Endogenous government behaviour: Wagner's Law or Gotterdamerung?' in Jackson and Cook 1979.

Chrystal K.A. and Alt J., 'Public sector behaviour: the status of the political business cycle,' Paper presented to AUTE Conference, Exeter, March 1979. Forthcoming in Conference Proceedings (1980).

Clower R., 'The Keynesian counter-revolution: a theoretical appraisal,' in Hahn F.H. and Brechling F.P.R. (eds), *The Theory of Interest Rates*, Macmillan, 1965.

Cripps F. and Godley W., 'A formal analysis of the Cambridge Economic Policy Group model,' *Economica*, November 1976.

Cripps F., Fetherston M. and Godley W., 'What is left of New Cambridge?' *Economic Policy Review*, March 1976.

Committee on the Working of the Monetary System, Report, Cmnd 827, HMSO, August 1959 (Radcliffe).

Committee on Policy Optimisation, Report, Cmnd 7148, HMSO, March 1978 (Ball).

Corden W.M., 'Exchange rate protection,' Paper presented to meeting of International Economics Study Group, 15 May 1978a. Mimeo, Trade Policy Research Centre.

Corden W.M., 'Exchange rate protection and the general equilibrium of nations,' Paper presented to annual conference of International Economics Study Group, September 1978b. Mimeo, Trade Policy Research Centre.

Davidson J.E.H. *et al.*, 'Econometric modelling of the aggregate time-series relationship between consumers' expenditure and income in the UK,' *Economic Journal*, December 1978. ,

Dornbusch R. and Fisher S., *Macroeconomics*, McGraw-Hill 1978.

Edgren G., Faxen K. and Ohdner C., 'Wages, growth and the distribution of income,' *Swedish Journal of Economics* 1969, pp. 133—60.

Eltis W., 'The failure of the Keynesian conventional wisdom,' *Lloyds Bank Review*, October 1976.

Evans M.K., *Macroeconomic Activity*, Harper and Row 1969.

Fetherston M.J., 'Estimation of simultaneous relationships: A UK private expenditure function,' Department of Applied Economics, University of Cambridge 1975.

Fetherston M.J. and Godley W.A.H., ' "New Cambridge" macroeconomics and global monetarism,' in Brunner and Meltzer 1978.

Fisher I., 'A statistical relation between unemployment and price changes,' *International Labour Review*, 1926; Reprinted in *Journal of Political Economy*, March/April 1973, pp. 596–602.

Frenkel J.A. and Johnson H.G. (eds), *The Monetary Approach to the Balance of Payments*, Allen and Unwin 1976.

Frenkel J.A. and Johnson H.G. (eds), *The Economics of Exchange Rates*, Addison-Wesley 1978.

Frey B., *Modern Political Economy*, Martin Robertson 1978.

Frey B. and Schneider F., 'A politico-economic model of the UK', *Economic Journal*, June 1978.

Friedman M., 'The role of monetary policy,' *American Economic Review*, March 1968.

Goldfeld S. and Blinder A., 'Some implications of endogenous stabilisation policy,' *Brooking Papers on Economic Activity* 1972.

Goodwin R.M., 'A growth cycle,' reprinted in Hunt E.K. and Schwartz J.G., *A Critique of Economic Theory*, Penguin 1972.

Gordon R.J., *Macroeconomics*, Little Brown 1978.

Green F. and Nore P. (eds), *Economics: An Anti-Text*, Martin Robertson 1977.

Hansen A., *A Guide to Keynes*, McGraw-Hill 1953.

Harris L., The balance of payments and the international economic system', in Green and Nore 1977.

Hendry D.F. and Mizon G.E., 'Serial correlation as a convenient simplification, not a nuisance', *Economic Journal*, September 1978.

Henry S.G.B and Ormerod P.A., 'Incomes policy and wage inflation: empirical evidence for the UK 1961–77,'NIESR Economic Review, August 1978, pp. 31–9.

Henry S.G.B., Sawyer M.C. and Smith P., 'Models of inflation in the UK: an evaluation.' *NIESR Economic Review*, August 1976, pp. 60–71.

Hicks J.R., 'Mr Keynes and the "classics": a suggested interpretation,' *Econometrica*, April 1937.

Hines A.G., 'Trade unions and wage inflation in the UK 1893–1960.' *Review of Economic Studies* 1964, pp. 221–52.

Hines A.G. and Catephores G., 'Investment in UK manufacturing industry,' in Hilton K., and Heathfield D.F., *The Econometric Study of the UK*, Macmillan 1970.

Jackson P.M. and Cook S.T. (eds), *Current Issues in Fiscal Policy*, Martin Robertson 1979.

Johnson H.G., 'The monetary approach to balance of payments theory,' in Frenkel and Johnson 1976.

Jonson P., 'A model of the UK balance of payments,'*Journal of Political Economy*, 1976.

Kahn, Lord, 'Thoughts on the behaviour of wages and monetarism,' *Lloyds Bank Review*, January 1976.

Kaldor N., 'The new monetarism,' *Lloyds Bank Review*, July 1970.

Kaldor N., 'Conflicts in national objectives,' *Economic Journal*, March 1971.

Krause L.B. and Salant W.S. (eds), *Worldwide Inflation: Theory and Recent Experience*, Brookings Institution 1977.

Laidler D.E.W., 'Inflation in Britain: a monetarist perspective', *American Economic Review*, September 1976.

Laidler D.E.W., 'Money and money income: an essay on the transmission mechanism,' *Journal of Monetary Economics*, 1978a.

Laidler D.E.W., 'A monetarist viewpoint,' in Posner 1978b.

Laury J.S.E., Lewis G.R., and Ormerod P.A., 'Properties of macroeconomic models of the UK economy: a comparative study,' *NIESR Economic Review*, February 1978.

Leijonhufvud A., *On Keynesian Economics and the Economics of Keynes*, Oxford University Press 1968.

Leijonhufvud A., 'Keynes and the classics,' *Institute of Economic Affairs Occasional Paper 30*, 1969.

Lewis G.R. and Ormerod P.A., 'Policy simulations and model characteristics,' in Jackson and Cook 1979.

Lipsey R.G., 'The relationship between unemployment and the rate of change of money wage rates in the UK 1862–1957: a further analysis,' *Economica*, 1960, pp. 1–31.

Lomax R. and Denham M., 'The model of external capital flows,' *Treasury Working Paper No. 8*, December 1978.

Macrae D., 'A political model of the business cycle,' *Journal of Political Economy* 1977.

Malinvaud E., *The Theory of Unemployment Reconsidered*, Basil Blackwell 1977.

Meade J.E. and Andrews P.W.S., 'Summary of replies to questions on the effects of interest rates,' in Wilson and Andrews 1951.

Miller M.H., 'Can a rise in import prices be inflationary and deflationary?' *American Economic Review*, September 1976.

Modigliani F., 'Liquidity preference and the theory of interest and money,' *Econometrica*, January 1944.

Modigliani F., 'The monetarist controversy or, should we forsake stabilization policy?' *American Economic Review*, March 1977.

Mundell R.A., *International Economics*, Macmillan 1968.

Muth J.F., 'Rational expectations and the theory of price movements,' *Econometrica*, July 1961.

Neild R.R. and Ward T.S., *The Measurement and Reform of Budgetary Policy*, Heinemann 1978.

Ninth Report from the Expenditure Committee, Session 1974, HC328, HMSO, July 1974.

Nordhaus W., 'The political business cycle,' *Review of Economic Studies* 1975.

Paldam M., 'Is there an electoral cycle? A study of national accounts,' Aarhus Institute of Economics, *Discussion Paper No. 8*, 1977.

Parkin M. and Sumner M.T. (eds), *Incomes Policy and Inflation*, Manchester University Press 1972.

Parkin M., 'Alternative explanations of UK inflation: a survey,' in Parkin and Sumner 1978.

Parkin M. and Sumner M.T. (eds), *Inflation in the UK*, Manchester University Press 1978.

Parkin M., Sumner M.T. and Jones R.A., 'A survey of the econometric evidence of the effects of incomes policy on the rate of inflation,' in Parkin and Sumner 1972.

Patinkin D., 'The Chicago tradition, the quantity theory and Friedman,' *Journal of Money Credit and Banking*, 1, 1969, pp. 46−70.

Peston M.H., *Theory of Macroeconomic Policy*, Philip Allan 1974.

Phelps E.S., 'Money-wage dynamics and labor market equilibrium,' *Journal of Political Economy*, July/August 1968.

Phillips A.W.H., 'The relation between unemployment and the rate of change of money wage rates in the UK 1861−1957,' *Economica*, November 1958, pp. 283−99.

Posner M. (ed.), *Demand Management*, Heinemann 1978.

Purdy D.L. and Zis G., 'Trade unions and wage inflation in the UK: a reappraisal,' in Parkin M. (ed.), *Essays in Modern Economics*, Longman 1973.

Rowan D.C., 'Godley's Law, Godley's Rule and New Cambridge macroeconomics,' Banca Nazionale del Lavoro *Quarterly Bulletin*, June 1976.

Sargent T.J., 'A classical macroeconomic model for the United States,' *Journal of Political Economy*, April 1976.

Sargent T.J. and Wallace N., ' "Rational" expectations, the optimal monetary instrument, and the optimal money supply rule,' *Journal of Political Economy*, April 1975.

Savage D., 'The channels of monetary influence: a survey of the empirical evidence,' *NIESR Economic Review*, February 1978.

Smith G.W., 'Price determination,' in Parkin and Sumner 1978.

Spencer P. and Mowl C., 'The model of the domestic monetary system,' *Treasury Working Paper No. 8*, December 1978.

Spencer R.W. and Yohe W.P., 'The "crowding out" of private expenditures by fiscal policy actions,' Federal Reserve Bank of St. Louis *Monthly Review*, October 1970.

Sraffa P., *Production of Commodities by Means of Commodities*, Cambridge University Press 1960.

Sumner M.T., 'Wage determination,' in Parkin and Sumner 1978.

Swoboda A.K., 'Monetary approaches to worldwide inflation.' in Krause and Salant 1977.

Tinbergen J., *On the Theory of Economic Policy*, North Holland 1952.

Townend J.C., 'The personal saving ratio,' Bank of England *Quarterly Bulletin*, March 1976.

Williamson J. and Wood G.E., 'The British inflation: indigenous or imported?' *American Economic Review* 1976, pp. 520−31.

Wilson T. and Andrews P.W.S., *Oxford Studies in the Price Mechanism*, Oxford University Press 1951.

Zellner A., Huang D.S. and Chau, L.C., 'Further analysis of the short-run consumption function with emphasis on the role of liquid assets,' *Econometrica*, July 1965.

Index

Alt J.E., 144, 154, 164, 165, 167, 168
Anderson L.C., 143
Andrews P.W.S., 62
Artis M.J., 84
Aukrust O., 137

Bacon R., 151–155
Balance of payments, 103–120
Ball Committee, 165
Ball R.J., 137, 165
Barro R.J., 70
Bean C., 7n
Beutel M., 53
Bispham J., 91
Blinder A., 85, 98–99, 114, 144
Branson W., 1
Brittan S., 114, 165, 167
Brunner K., 149
Burns T., 137

Cambridge Economic Policy
    Group, 74, 88–100, 186
    aggregate expenditure function,
        92–97
    balance of payments, 112–114
    import controls, 113
    inflation, 97, 136
    stabilisation, 159
Cambridge equation, 75
Carlson K.M., 143
Catephores G., 63

Chau L.C., 30
Chrystal K.A., 144, 154, 164,
    167, 168
Clower R. 68
Consumption, 29
Corden M., 178
Cripps F., 88–100
Crowding out, 142–155

Davidson J.E.H., 30
Denham M., 45
Dornbusch R., 1

Edgren G., 137
Eltis W., 67, 151–155
Evans M.K., 46n, 181
Exchange rate, 114
Exchange rate protection, 177
Exports, 33

Faxen K., 137
Fetherston M.J., 90, 92, 95,
    114
Fisher I., 123
Fisher S., 1
Frenkel J.A., 115
Frey B., 165, 167
Friedman M., 73, 75, 78–79,
    125, 143, 146

Godley W.A.H., 88–100, 114
Goldfeld S., 144

Goodwin R.M., 160
Gordon R.J., 1, 126, 134, 156,
    157, 185
Green F., 53
Grossman H., 70

Hansen A., 58
Harris L., 54
Harrod R., 67
Hawtrey X., 143
Hendry D.F., 84
Henry S.G.B., 136, 139
Hicks J.R., 15
Hines A.G., 63, 124, 136
Huang D.S., 30

Imports, 34
Incomes policy, 138–140
Inflation, 40, 121–141
Investment, 31
Invisibles, 35

Johnson H.G., 110, 115
Jones R.A., 138
Jonson P., 79
Jordan J.L., 143

Kahn, Lord, 66, 67
Kaldor N., 67, 85, 89
Keynes J.M., 15, 145
Keynesian approach to balance
    of payments, 103
Keynesians, 57–72, 74, 85

Laidler D.E.W., 80–82, 85,
    125, 160–161, 172
Laury J.S.E., 29, 46n
Leijonhufvud A., 68
Lewis G.R., 29, 64n, 150
Lewis M.K., 84
Lipsey R.G., 123, 136
Litvack H., 1
Lomax R., 45
London Business School, 28, 43
    137, 181

Macmillan Committee, 143
Macrae D., 167

Malinvaud E., 70
Meade J.E., 62
Meltzer A.H., 149
Miller M.H., 170, 172
Mizon G.E., 84
Modigliani F., 63, 85, 156, 157,
    162
Monetarism, 73–87, 160–162
Monetary approach to balance
    of payments, 108
Money demand, 83
Mowl C., 7n, 45
Mundell R.A., 105

National Institute, 28, 43
Natural rate of unemployment, 81
Neild R.R., 89, 90, 91
New Cambridge, see Cambridge
    Economic Policy Group
Nore P., 53
North Sea oil, 175–177

Ohdner C., 137
Oil crisis, 169–175
Okun's Law, 130
Optimal control, 163–165
Ormerod P.A., 29, 46n, 139, 150

Parkin J.M., 136, 138, 140
Phelps E.S., 125
Phillips A.W., 123
Phillips curve, 84, 123–125,
    128–134, 181, 184
Pigou, 75
Pigou effect, 78
Purdy D.L., 124

Quantity theory, 74

Radcliffe Report, 67
Radical economists, 52–55
Rational expectations, 81, 162
Real balance effect, 77
Robertson D.H., 75
Rowan D.C., 93

Sargent T.J., 82, 85, 162
Savage D., 63

Scandinavian model, 136–138, 152
Schneider F., 165, 167
Smith, Adam, 143, 152
Spencer P., 7n, 45
Spencer R.W., 143
Sraffa P., 56n
Sumner M.T., 138

Theil H., 163
Tinbergen J., 163
Townend J.C., 79

Treasury model, 2, 18, 28–46, 79, 115, 123, 150, 181

Unemployment, 38, 121–141

Wallace N., 82, 85, 102
Ward T.S., 91
Worswick G.D.N., 122, 170

Yohe W.P., 143

Zellner A., 30
Zis G., 124